Losing a Parent

Fiona Marshall has written widely on health and psychology. She is also a fiction author.

Overcoming Common Problems Series

Selected titles

A full list of titles is available from Sheldon Press on our website at
www.sheldonpress.co.uk

The A to Z of Eating Disorders
Emma Woolf

Autism and Asperger Syndrome in Adults
Dr Luke Beardon

Chronic Pain the Drug-free Way
Phil Sizer

Coping with Aggressive Behaviour
Dr Jane McGregor

Coping with Diverticulitis
Peter Cartwright

Coping with Headaches and Migraine
Alison Frith

Coping with the Psychological Effects of Illness
Dr Fran Smith, Dr Carina Eriksen and Professor Robert Bor

Dementia Care: A guide
Christina Macdonald

Depression and Anxiety the Drug-free Way
Mark Greener

Depressive Illness: The curse of the strong
Dr Tim Cantopher

Dr Dawn's Guide to Sexual Health
Dr Dawn Harper

Dr Dawn's Guide to Toddler Health
Dr Dawn Harper

Dr Dawn's Guide to Your Baby's First Year
Dr Dawn Harper

Dying for a Drink: All you need to know to beat the booze
Dr Tim Cantopher

The Empathy Trap: Understanding antisocial personalities
Dr Jane McGregor and Tim McGregor

Everything Your GP Doesn't Have Time to Tell You about Alzheimer's
Dr Matt Piccaver

Everything Your GP Doesn't Have Time to Tell You about Arthritis
Dr Matt Piccaver

Gestational Diabetes: Your survival guide to diabetes in pregnancy
Dr Paul Grant

The Heart Attack Survival Guide
Mark Greener

The Holistic Guide for Cancer Survivors
Mark Greener

Hope and Healing after Stillbirth and New Baby Loss
Professor Kevin Gournay and Dr Brenda Ashcroft

How to Stop Worrying
Dr Frank Tallis

IBS: Dietary advice to calm your gut
Alex Gazzola and Julie Thompson

Living with Angina
Dr Tom Smith

Living with Multiple Sclerosis
Mark Greener

Living with Tinnitus and Hyperacusis
Dr Laurence McKenna, Dr David Baguley and Dr Don McFerran

Mental Health in Children and Young People: Spotting symptoms and seeking help early
Dr Sarah Vohra

The Multiple Sclerosis Diet Book
Tessa Buckley

Parenting Your Disabled Child: The first three years
Margaret Barrett

Sleep Better: The science and the myths
Professor Graham Law and Dr Shane Pascoe

Stress-related Illness
Dr Tim Cantopher

Taming the Beast Within: Understanding personality disorder
Professor Peter Tyrer

Therapy Pets: A guide
Jill Eckersley

Toxic People: Dealing with dysfunctional relationships
Dr Tim Cantopher

Treating Arthritis: The drug-free way
Margaret Hills and Christine Horner

Treating Arthritis Diet Book
Margaret Hills

Understanding Hoarding
Jo Cooke

Vertigo and Dizziness
Jaydip Ray

Wellbeing: Body confidence, health and happiness
Emma Woolf

Your Guide for the Cancer Journey: Cancer and its treatment
Mark Greener

Lists of titles in the Mindful Way and Sheldon Short Guides series are also available from Sheldon Press.

Overcoming Common Problems

Losing a Parent

Second edition

FIONA MARSHALL

First published in Great Britain in 1993
Second edition published 2011

This edition published by Sheldon Press in 2020
An imprint of John Murray Press
A division of Hodder & Stoughton Ltd,
An Hachette UK company

3

A CIP catalogue record for this title is available from the British Library

Trade Paperback ISBN 9781529381061
eBook ISBN 9781529352511

Typeset by Cenveo® Publisher Services.

Printed and bound in Great Britain by Clays Ltd, Elcograf S.p.A.

John Murray Press policy is to use papers that are natural, renewable and
recyclable products and made from wood grown in sustainable forests.
The logging and manufacturing processes are expected to conform to the
environmental regulations of the country of origin.

John Murray Press
Carmelite House
50 Victoria Embankment
London EC4Y 0DZ

www.sheldonpress.co.uk

To M

Contents

Introduction

We tend to believe that our mother and father will never die. Even if a long illness gives us time to prepare ourselves, we can never be fully ready for their death and its aftermath, which means saying goodbye to the people who gave us life, apart from anything else. No matter what our age, the death of a parent is devastating; nothing else leaves us feeling so abandoned. Not only do we lose a much-loved individual, we also face a severe identity crisis because that person was so much part of ourselves and our past. Also, our mother's or our father's death is often our first close encounter with death and means coming to terms with our own mortality in a very real sense. Life as we have known it stops and we are left in the deep isolation of grief; we are forced to work through this and there are no short cuts, if we are eventually to recover emotional health. This work of grief, which can take years, covers many aspects of our lives: we have to consider our parent's life in a totally new light – to accept him or her as vulnerable, to assimilate this loss of a part of ourselves, and to formulate some concept of death.

This need to find meaning in what has happened can transform pain into valuable insights with which to face the rest of our lives. The subject of this book is how to find this meaning; how to see, eventually, your mother's or father's death as the beginning of a new strength and maturity.

It's a book needed all the more because the loss of a mother or father seems to be one of society's invisible areas – or at least, semi-visible ones. Like disabled people and struggling young mothers, dying parents have always been there; they blend into the background, unless you happen to be one of them or closely connected with one of them. The general attitude (felt if not expressed) seems to be that, although it is a highly upsetting event, the loss of a parent is more or less to be expected. Condolences tend to skim over the profound psychological effects this event can have. After all, you're an adult, aren't you? Thus, the isolation which is a normal feature of bereavement is accentuated.

Thanks to media coverage of disasters and post-traumatic stress, there *is* far more public awareness of the damage that can be caused by unresolved grief, and it seems that more people are going to bereavement support groups. Many of these do come to discuss the death of their mother or father; indeed, very often, people who come to bereavement support groups, ostensibly to discuss the loss of a partner, really need to talk about the unassimilated, earlier loss of a parent. Could it be a comment on our culture, which puts so much emphasis on couples, that so many bereavement studies are done on the widowed? In comparison, the death of a parent and its effects on the adult child is a 'poor relation', according to research. Add to this our society's taboo on death and you realize that a person bereaved of a father or mother may be very lonely indeed.

I hope this book will go some way towards helping if not curing that loneliness: those who read it will know at least that it is a shared loneliness. Having been through the event myself, I appreciate not only this isolation, but the need of a bereaved person to make sense of what has happened. Grieving can be a long process, especially if you need to formulate some personal philosophy of death – incorporating both parents, dead or alive, into the framework of a reasonably contented and mature life.

Generally, the younger you are, the harder you are likely to be hit by the death of a parent. But there are many other factors which affect grieving. If you are heavily involved with other life events, such as getting married or having a baby, mourning may be delayed or complicated. Equally, if you are advanced in life and have been used to having your parents around, perhaps even looking after them, their loss can be a blow which turns your life upside-down. It is by no means uncommon for people of 60 or more to feel that they are orphans, alone in the world. Nevertheless, the death of your mother or father is part of the natural sequence of events: that is, parents do most often die before their children. In some ways, their death also frees their adult children to take on responsibilities and roles they might not otherwise have accepted. The bereaved are now the leading generation; they have inherited mentally, culturally and perhaps in material terms as well. Though frightening, this can form eventually a challenge which many find liberating.

But, while the trend of this book is towards growth and recovery, it is also important to remember that meaning cannot be forced. Death cannot always be mentally 'tidied up' by all the coping strategies that come to us from religion and other sources, and letting go of what has happened is a vital part of recovery, with all its pain, its raggedness and its imperfection. The ambulance which didn't come in time, the doctor who was offhand, the priest who was less than pastoral – these may always hurt, but cannot be clung to if we are to become sound again. It is easier if we can accept that letting go comes with time, and that it may never be total: no one will ever be complacent about the way Dad died, or regard it as neatly fitting in with the universe's master plan. Pain and grief may have ultimate value; for now it is enough to say that this value, if transcendent, is certainly not tidy! Try to make sense of what has happened, beyond a certain point, and we always risk being confounded.

Finally, the way you go through any bereavement also depends on the quality of your relationship with the person who has died. Few parent–child relationships are likely to have been completely smooth. A certain amount of inter-generation conflict is inevitable, even healthy. But death, which may not have left time to put the relationship on a more settled footing, does not necessarily end this relationship. As the years go by, hopefully there will be time enough to reach a greater understanding of your mother or father, and a more total acceptance of the way they lived as well as the way they died.

How this book is arranged

Everyone's experience is different, but by including a number of case histories, I hope that the book will touch on as many reactions as possible, and that talking about genuine people will make the book seem more real. The people interviewed were drawn from as wide a range of ages and social backgrounds as possible.

It is all too easy for a writer to hide out in pseudo-technical bereavement language, which doesn't really help a grieving person and can even add to the feeling of unreality we tend to experience in mourning. For this reason, I have tried deliberately to avoid using psychological terms such as 'searching' (a reaction shortly after death which involves going round the house looking for or expecting to see the dead person). As many people's parents today die of one kind of lingering disease or another, the book opens with what is really the beginning of death: hearing the news, or realizing for yourself that your mother or father is dying. Death *itself* is considered after this, with a separate section on sudden death, which can cause a different reaction where shock plays a much greater part.

Grief is looked at next in great detail: immediate grief, covering the first two years; and the factors which can complicate or prolong it. It is important to look beyond this, however – the 'coming through' grief and life beyond must both be acknowledged. It isn't just that parental influences have a way of haunting us for life, but that we may miss the person we have lost in far more situations, for far longer than we anticipate. As we progress further towards maturity ourselves, the death of our mother or father continues to need us to come to terms with our grief.

Note: I refer sometimes to 'father' and sometimes to 'mother', but they are intended to be interchangeable and it is hoped that they will be read as such.

1

Terminal illness: anticipating death

Hazel, a 30-year-old cashier in a building society, had been waiting all day for her mother Barbara to return from the hospital where her father was suffering from bowel cancer. Barbara returned at last in the late afternoon.

> She asked me to make her a cup of tea, which I thought faintly odd because she always did her own. When she had it she sat down. She told me that my father had had his operation. I asked how he was and she said, 'Well, weak.' Then she said that the consultant had had a word with her. All the doctors had done was open him up and then sew him up again because they saw at once that the cancer was in fact inoperable. The doctor said it was only a matter of a couple of months now.

Nothing can soften the shock of hearing that your mother or father is dying. Even if you already had your suspicions, another person's voice confirming your private fears can all too easily be felt as an intrusion – even a violation. There is a long-established hatred for the bearer of bad news, the harbinger of doom; when the news is broken to you, you understand that this hatred is very real, even when whoever tells you has done his or her best to be tactful and kindly.

In particular, doctors are used to dealing with anger from relatives of a dying person; depending on the circumstances, you may well hear the news from someone in the medical profession. If, for example, one or both of your parents are failing and elderly, you will probably be viewed by doctors as the most appropriate person to be told. However, many people hear about their parent's condition from another family member, often your other parent. Thus, there is also the shock of seeing family personas break down – an unshakeable aunt in tears, a nonchalant brother silenced. Worst of all is the reaction of your other parent. Up to now, he or she may have been a tower of strength, or at least a known factor whose strengths and weaknesses were familiar, even set pieces. Now, familiarity is destroyed, roles break down and disorientation sets in. Life now enters a strange state of suspension which consists of waiting for death; a harrowing time during which it is possible to experience the gamut of reactions from peace to searing pain.

For now, your body may respond before your mind does, with your most immediate reaction on hearing the news producing physical symptoms: cold, clammy hands, feelings of heaviness, giddiness and sickness, the need to go to the toilet very often, or sudden diarrhoea. You can help this shock pass away by keeping warm and quiet, and drinking hot, sweet fluids, preferably non-alcoholic. It may seem unbearably trivial even to think of these things at such a moment, but for many reasons it is necessary to look after yourself from the very beginning of this life experience.

In the first place, obvious though it may sound, you have to go on living. You will not function properly unless you make a conscious effort to eat and sleep properly during the extremely stressful time that lies ahead. As you will see later, bereavement is a prime time for ill health to strike because the stress of grieving lowers your resistance to infection – and if you can help ward this off by your own efforts, all well and good. Physical illness is not only debilitating in itself; it also paves the way for prolonged, negative mental reactions. Depression is one example, whether it's post-influenza blues or the washed-out feeling which comes after a tummy bug. Morbidity can be another reaction. If, for example, you have neglected to eat properly for some months, and have lost weight, it can be easy to feel that you are beginning to look skeletal and on the way to death yourself. Anorexia could be a related problem, in this kind of circumstance, or just the feeling that you are unattractive and not worth bothering about. Generally, if your parent has died of some disease, you are likely to be more anxious about any illness which strikes you, and to give it undue importance. Taking care of yourself helps you to protect yourself from such exaggerated long-term reactions, though most grieving people will be touched by them – you can only do so much. It is quite normal to feel a bewildering range of emotions.

Also, you need to be strong both in order to support your parent and other members of your family if need be and, most importantly, in order to know when to switch off and find some sort of relaxation. People outside a family where a parent is dying, and sometimes the dying parents themselves, can sometimes feel hurt and shocked at the way the children take time off, perhaps spending a day in the country or an evening at the cinema, apparently forgetting all about their parents' plight – but this is vital.

Following the initial shock, disbelief may set in; the conviction that the doctor has made a mistake, that your father will show his accustomed strength of character and pull through, or that the doctor is wrong because he or she doesn't know your father as well as you do and the simple feeling that it is not in the nature of your parents to die. This feeling is what makes losing a mother or father different from other close bereavements: the childish conviction that they are betraying their responsibility as your caretakers by dying. No matter how mature you are, it is worth trying to come to terms with this childish centre in yourself because it will save you much later anger at your 'selfishness'.

Once disbelief has passed off – though it may flood in again and again for a long time after the initial shock – other reactions begin to mingle. Anger, a very common part of bereavement, can strike before death too, taking unexpected and upsetting forms. It may be directed not just at the perceived incompetence of doctors, or at God, but at your sick father for daring to die in the first place, especially if you have some important event coming up, such as a new job.

You may then start to try and control the event in your head; wanting your father to wait for a marriage, the birth of a child, or for just a few more months of life. At the same time, you may also wish death to take place quickly. This wretched waiting, during which time you want both to hang on to your father and speed him on his way, can be a time of great confusion.

Anger may also be felt at your other parent for imposing a fatal life-style on his or her partner – for not making him give up smoking or drinking, for example, or simply for not taking enough care of her.

Michael was a 35-year-old mechanic whose mother spent several months a year in her native America. He felt that his father Tom, who was 72, was dying partly because his mother hadn't been around to take proper care of him. Good food and prompt medical attention might have given him a few more years of life – had his mother been there to make sure it was administered.

This anger at the other parent, complicated by guilt at that other parent's grief, is very real, however irrational. All you can do is to be aware of it but to try not to take it too much to heart – it will pass.

You may also have to cope not just with your own reactions, but with those of siblings or other family members. As you will read later in the book, this is a great time for family discord – for all those buried childhood resentments to rise, for you to forget to treat siblings as the adults they now are, or to endure some such forgetting yourself.

Michael had three older brothers with whom he had an uneasy relationship. He felt he had always been patronized by the elder two, and despised outright by the other one, with the sentiment more than returned! The brothers had little in common and, at the time of Tom's death, had been engaged in family tensions and disputes.

Generally, there's all the tension of having to deal in an adult way with an event which can easily return you to childhood status again. However, not everyone experiences this kind of upset; some families do cope better than others, depending on the maturity of the individual members and their relationships, and can find themselves acting together all the way through their shared experience.

> Stephen, who had two brothers and one sister, was able to share the responsibilities brought about by his mother's death in a practical, trouble-free way. 'It was an utterly rotten time, but we all felt we just had to get on with it. There was no tension among us.'

Relief can be another reaction, especially if your father has been ailing for some time. To give up your own increasingly fruitless struggles with hope, to know that his suffering will end, makes this relief undeniable. Deep down, the exciting thought of true independence may also flash in: 'Now at last I'll be able to see what it's like to be on my own.' Naturally, guilt at such a feeling is likely to pour in, opening the floodgates for the guilt of a lifetime – all the neglected opportunities, all the parental love that wasn't quite returned, all the times you were angry with your parent in the past and all the times you and your brothers and sisters may have 'ganged up' against parental authority. The natural ambivalence involved in the parent–child relationship makes this guilt strong and durable.

Fear is one of the most isolating and draining emotions of this time, though this partly depends on how much prior experience you have had of death. Someone who has had to cope with the death of a grandparent – or an aunt, uncle or family pet – is better prepared for the fact of death, although this doesn't take away the intense emotional reactions. A parent's death can be seen as the beginning of your own: the first pull of yourself towards that great darkness. It strikes home with real force: if Mum or Dad can die then so can I! The implications of this are something which have to be worked through for a long time during bereavement.

Apart from this basic fear, you may also be afraid of being with your dying father or of being present at the moment of death and afterwards. These are natural fears in a society where most individuals have very little experience of death. Even if you have had experience of other family members dying, a mother or father is usually closer to home in every sense of the word. You may not even have seen the body of your grandmother who died when you were 20; you may now be faced with the prospect of being with your father in his last moments. As with all fear, though, it is often more unpleasant beforehand than on the day itself. Being present at death can actually be a source of peace and relief. (See Chapter 3 for more on the moment of death.)

These feelings, though strong, are not always easy to identify: you may feel confused or simply blank. Be gentle with yourself; unfortunately there is no short cut through the trauma of grief. Grief is not an illness, but it does have to be lived through in order to find growth and peace eventually.

'Telling' – who tells whom about imminent death

The way in which the news of imminent death is broken can be profoundly revealing of a family's lifelong ethos and relationships, and can have far-reaching repercussions. It touches on the core of the parent–child relationship – whether trusting, evasive, calm or conflict-ridden – and is a major test of communication within the family.

> Guy, 21, knew his father was ill but not how seriously ill. As he was taking his final exams at university, his family felt he should be shielded from the reality of his father's cancer. In the event, his aunt, who strongly disagreed, took matters in her hands and rang Guy to tell him the truth. Guy returned home to find that the consultant had just given his father three weeks to live. This proved to be right almost to the day and left Guy very little time to assimilate the news or prepare for the event. Guy experienced great anger at his family in wishing to 'protect' him in this way – he felt that although he was technically adult, he was still considered too young to know.

Guy's story highlights one of the aspects of a father or mother's death – the sense of exclusion that can result if the 'adult' members of the family decide to keep the news to themselves. Guy found these 'adult lies' all the more frustrating because his local hospital had a good team which could have offered not only frankness but support and counselling. After his father's death, he found it more difficult to support his mother because she followed up her previous lack of openness by bottling up her feelings and could not confide in him at all. This method of 'telling' also made Guy re-examine his parents' values and his relationship with them very carefully. Guy concluded there was a history of non-communication, too much emphasis on academic success and that in general he had been 'told too little' all his life.

The right way to be told

Ultimately there is no right way. It is also true, if much depends on inter-family relationships, that sometimes the news does not need telling. Death is there, for all to see – words become superfluous.

However, given the fact that so many people today spend time in hospital before dying, what about the role of doctors (and their colleagues) when it comes to breaking the news of oncoming death? Hospitals these days do tend towards greater openness in the face of death, although some professionals consider there is still a long way to go. In an ideal situation, however, your hospital would have a multi-disciplinary team consisting of doctors, nurses, occupational therapists, physiotherapists, counsellors and social workers. Regular meetings would decide at which point the team felt that a patient's disease was incurable, and how to go about telling the sick person and/or his family. In this way, you could be sure that any information would be given in a thought-out, sensitive manner.

However, in smaller organizations, it may well just be up to the personality of the individual doctor on call at that moment as to how and how much you are told. Even in large hospitals, with a well-organized team, there is no best or recognized way of breaking this news because it depends so much on the nature of each dying person. In theory, it might make sense for the sick person to be told first, and then the family. But, for example, it is difficult to tell the truth to someone who vehemently denies that he is ill and insists he is getting better – much of telling depends on how willing, or how capable, the listener is to hear. Sometimes, even with the best efforts, it is impossible for a dying person or a relative to take in the news. It may be necessary to return as many as six or seven times to ask the same questions.

Additionally, the doctor *may* be awkward at telling. Although doctors do now have some training in death counselling, this may not be put into practice at once and can easily get swamped under the rest of their work. But it isn't just a matter of the individual personality of the doctor: it can be easy to mis-hear or misunderstand what the doctor is saying. For example, a doctor says, 'Things don't look good but there is always something we can do.' The doctor may go off believing he has imparted the news of impending death. You may leave believing that a cure is possible whereas the doctor has been speaking in terms of making the sick person more comfortable during his last weeks of life.

Getting information about your parent's condition can be more difficult if, like Guy, your parents have been told but aren't willing to tell you. The doctor has done his duty and, like the rest of his team, is probably too busy to seek out somebody who might need help. However, if you are confused, or if you fear the worst but can't get straight answers from your family, it is possible to ask someone else for help – probably the best person would be the hospital social worker or chaplain. Ethically, of course, he or she cannot divulge private information about a patient, but he might be able to advise on how to break a communication barrier with your parents.

Treatment and relationships with the medical profession

As already mentioned, it is easy to be unclear about what medical treatment your father is receiving. Doctors are used to hearing conflicting messages from the relatives of a dying person who are unable to bear the fact of death coming in its own way, in its own time. 'Can't you give him something to speed it up?' may be followed hours or even minutes later by, 'Why haven't you tried something that would give him a few more comfortable months?'

It's a time of great confusion: waiting for the end, wanting it to be over, yet desperate to hang on to your father for as long as possible. Not only is it hard to accept our own lack of authority in the face of death but it is also possible that we transfer to the doctor some of our parent's status. He or she can, for a while, become a substitute parent or authority figure, which makes it harder to accept that he or she doesn't have the answer.

The 'mechanics' of a hospital can also make it difficult to keep up with what is going on. Doctors and nurses change shifts – and a patient's condition does sometimes change very quickly, especially if he's in intensive care.

> Julia, a 40-year-old childminder, was called into hospital with the news that her father, Martin, was dying. Martin, 77, had just had a successful operation for cancer of the pancreas but now Julia and her family were told that drugs to relieve him of excess water weren't working. But, even as the family were being given tea and sympathy by the staff, another doctor came on and decided to do some more X-rays. These gave a completely different diagnosis and new drugs were tried – with amazing success. Martin left hospital two weeks later to recoup in a nursing home, and lived on for another four years after that.

If you're not sure what is going on in terms of diagnosis and treatment, you should feel free to go back and discuss this with the doctors – it can sometimes just be hard to take the facts in.

Your mother or father may well want to discuss choices of treatment with you. This can be a chance to listen to any fears she or he may have. For example, she may be afraid of being left alone or in pain, of being a burden, of suffering a long drawn-out death or of losing control. It is worth noting that generally, older people have fewer death fears than younger – they've accomplished more, have fewer plans for the future, and, if they've been seriously ill before, may even feel that they're living on borrowed time, especially if their spouse or friends have already passed away.

Moira's mother, for example, had no fears of death itself – it was the death process she hated, with all its petty indignities and suffering. She managed to live a fairly full life for some years after her illness was diagnosed, but recurrent crises in her health exhausted her and it was finally felt that she was relieved to die.

There may also be times when you feel that the choice of managing your parent's last days is an obvious one.

Hazel's father, now unconscious, was about to die, as it had been established that the cancer had spread widely within his body. He had lost a great deal of weight and was indeed almost skeletal. The consultant gently told Hazel's family that he could put him on a drip, but that it would just prolong the situation for a few days. Following this hint, the family agreed to leave the drip, and appreciated Hazel's father being allowed to die in this way.

Where to die?

At some point you need to consider the practical options of hospital, hospice or home. Many people would prefer to die at home but don't want to be a burden on their families; it isn't everyone who can afford to take time off work to care for a sick parent, or to pay someone else to do so. Nor is it uncommon for families to be scared of the responsibility. However, while having a parent die at home is an obvious stress, those who do go ahead often report positive feelings afterwards. One point to be considered is if you have children in the house. Including them in the death can be healthy – if you are not too anxious about it. It's the secrecy which can trouble children together with the horrible imaginings of their own mind. Seeing Gran in her last 'sleep' may take much of the terror of death away. On the other hand, if your parent needs a lot of nursing, or is in pain, you may well feel that this is not an experience you want to share with your children. You do need to be strong to consider this option, even with the medical support you would have. Some people are simply too ill to be cared for at home. In addition, hospital can seem safe and reassuring; there are staff on call and some patients settle down to the ward routine contentedly enough, forging links with the nurses and doctors and perhaps being proud of being a 'good' patient.

> Anita's mother, Yvonne, became something of the ward 'pet'; someone that the nurses always stopped to pass the time of day with, and who always managed a bit of repartee in reply. Although in some ways a difficult and temperamental woman, she did have charm, and Anita felt that the staff were genuinely saddened when Yvonne died.

A hospice is more likely to include the family when it comes to treatment and pain relief. There may well be more open acceptance of death; many people have spoken or written about the peaceful, even happy atmosphere that can exist. The extra involvement can be helpful in starting to deal with your grief, and many hospices offer bereavement support groups (as do some hospitals). Most of all, a hospice can offer real peace and dignity to your parent; an assurance that to be dying is not to be written off, that life still has value and meaning. It can be a relief for your mother or father not to be in a hospital, where the emphasis is on curing, but in a place where death is faced openly. This doesn't have to mean a brave, smiling acceptance of death the minute you walk through the door. Indeed, one of the positive aspects of a hospice, from your parent's point of view, is that he may be more able to get in touch with and express all the feelings of anger, grief and fear that he may have felt obliged to hide up to now. In a hospice, the emphasis is on quality of life until death takes place, with pain control and individual care often making this a far more vital time than could have been hoped for.

Care at home

Whether or not your parent dies at home, there may well be times during the course of an illness when he needs to be cared for at home. The giving of this care is conditioned by how much help that parent is willing to accept from a child, even when that child is adult. Some parents are unwilling to let go of their position of authority and may want to oversee the running of the house, directing their care from their beds. Yvonne, for example, would even tell her daughter Anita what brand of soap powder to buy!

Nursing your parent requires all the tact, strength and detachment you can muster. You need to cultivate the awareness of when to offer a drink and when to refrain, when to speak and when to be silent. Sometimes you will do the wrong thing unintentionally – like drawing the curtains when the sick person wanted them open; a minor oversight which may anger, not the sick person, but your other parent, who sometimes can't help taking out overwrought feelings on you. You need to help your other parent without being obtrusive; to care for your dying parent at the same time as allowing him to maintain what independence he has. Above all, you should maintain a balance between the need for normality in your life, and the special pressures caused by the sickness of your parent.

If you can have some share in these, no matter how small, it will at least give some extra purpose to your days with a sick parent at home. With one room designated as sickroom, and nurses and doctors coming and going, the house will change its familiar character. It is easier if you can accept this and be part of it. You might, for example, like to arrange the sickroom for your parent, with a special trolley table for books, drinks and medicines; some new bedwear might well be appreciated, especially if your sick parent has lost a lot of weight. Often, very ill people don't want mirrors around – Michael's father Tom specifically asked for his to be taken away as he couldn't bear the sight of himself after losing so much weight.

The sickroom will probably be a bedroom but sometimes your parent may need one that is on the ground floor or nearer the bathroom. If your other parent now has to sleep in a spare bedroom, perhaps a few flowers could go in there, too.

Have to hand the phone numbers of hospital, doctors and advice and support groups. Make sure you get time out of the house, and share the care with other family members (see below). Finally, follow any medical instructions carefully, especially when it comes to pain relief, which may depend on absolutely regular application to be effective.

No room at the hospital?

One of the most frightening aspects of having a sick parent today is the possibility that he or she may not even be admitted to hospital because of bed shortages.

Michael had a real struggle to get his father into the local hospital, which was due to close – in fact, Tom was one of the last patients.

Michael felt it was only by losing his temper that he got Tom any attention at all – the staff was minimal and morale was obviously low.

In fact, Michael's whole experience of hospital was associated with pain and indignity, starting with an insensitive ambulance driver who expressed his doubts about whether the hospital would let Tom in all the way to A&E.

Incidentally, the same kind of thoughtlessness was experienced by Stephen when he took a taxi to his father's funeral – the taxi driver was obviously prepared to talk all the way about how hardened he was to funerals except when he saw the small white coffins which meant a child. Both Michael and Stephen had no hesitation in shutting up their respective tormentors. Stephen also rang the local taxi-cab service to complain about their driver's self-admitted callousness, pointing out that someone who was more overwhelmed by grief might have been more of a prey to it. There is certainly no need to bear with this level of conversation in tolerant silence.

Visiting in hospital

Seeing your parent in the depersonalized setting of the hospital can be disturbing. It isn't so much the utilitarian beds or the sterile cleanliness as the fact that your parent has been taken out of his natural setting and is at other people's mercy, no longer the authority figure. It's the stripping of dignity – seeing your parent connected to tubes, or in pain or distress. As Moira put it:

> I hated seeing my mother naked – both mentally and physically. I couldn't feel that it was right for a mother to lose all her privacy in front of her child.

And Michael, like many others, found it heart-breaking to see his father so afraid in hospital – partly an old man's fear of being moved from home and partly the fear of death.

> I remember when I saw my father at home the last time, he still had his spirit. It was after that dreadful medical examination just after he'd been admitted – they'd run out of veins to put a drip in and Tom kept struggling and shouting. He came out of the side-ward terrified, and kept clinging to me and asking me to stay. He was wheeled away down the corridor and I knew he didn't want to go, and was fighting every inch of the way. That was the last time I saw him conscious.

Michael's father, a strong-willed man, was not one to accept death lightly in any case – as will be discussed in the next chapter, people often die in the same spirit as they have lived.

The danger of over-empathizing should be mentioned here – perhaps attributing to a parent more pain and sensitivity than is in fact the case, or perhaps having your own objectivity clouded by your own pain. It can be very hard to admit to ourselves that our parent may want to go, that his readiness for his death is different from ours. While no one would want to deny the very real nature of Tom's suffering, Michael did later wonder if he hadn't overreacted slightly, whether he hadn't to some extent been projecting his own acute feelings of distress on to his father.

> Maybe he did want to go and it was me who didn't want to admit it. I blame the hospital partly for that, all the medical apparatus, the attitude of the doctors, it all seemed to get between us. How can either of you really tell what the other one's thinking in an atmosphere like that, where they're half-pretending they're going to cure him and they don't really care?

Michael didn't manage to make any rapports among the constantly changing and (he felt) indifferent staff of a large and busy hospital. He was also appalled at the hospital priest, whom he felt to be callous, unprofessional and tardy. But, as this is a time of such sensitivity, remember that it can be hard for anyone to say just the right thing. Every well-meant comment can grate, and a question about your father's religious beliefs or practices can seem like a gross and irrelevant intrusion. It has also to be said that Michael, like Tom, was a restless spirit, far readier to pick a quarrel with his comforters than to derive comfort from them. All unsatisfactory encounters can be sharper and more arid in the hospital setting, without the 'muffling familiarity' of home, especially if as often happens you know your parent will not leave the ward again.

But it does help if you can talk to someone during this time of waiting. It's true that help may not come automatically, and that you may have to ask. At this stage, the doctor doesn't have to be the obvious person any longer – perhaps you don't need authoritative knowledge so much as someone who understands. (This isn't to say that doctors don't understand, of course!) A doctor can also help by giving what is often a fairly accurate estimate of how much time remains. (Although many people can and do defy the 'six-months-to-live' prophecies, medical experience can gauge it better when it's a question of weeks or days.) But, you may also have managed to make friends with someone who has just happened to be around for more time than a busy consultant – a nurse, a cleaner, another patient, or another patient's family. Your father may also have made his own friends among the staff, who may visit of their own accord and will be able to share some of your fear and sorrow as death comes closer. Although Michael's negative experience has been described, there are many people who speak of the dedication and care of the staff they knew with heartfelt gratitude.

Hazel experienced sensitivity and tact in her dealings with the hospital team which cared for her father. Moira felt that, although the system was degrading, the individuals within the hospital were doing their best, often against the odds.

Other aspects of illness can make hospital visiting distressing, such as body odour, which can linger in the memory even after leaving the hospital. Guy, seeing his father in hospital for the first time in six weeks, was shocked at how much he had changed physically.

His face had gone sharp – it had always been thin, but now you could really see his cheekbones. His breathing was noisier. And he seemed to have a kind of glaze over his eyes – when he looked at me, it was as if he wasn't really seeing me, as if he couldn't.

2

You and your dying parent

The relationship with a dying mother or father needs careful reappraisal in the final months and weeks of life, as the past and the future rush together with ever-decreasing possibilities. How do you behave with your dying mother? Should oncoming death make such a difference anyway – isn't it better to act normally as far as possible? Should you try and talk to your mother about death? These are among the most difficult questions that you will ever have to face.

Generally, doctors agree that the dying person leads the way when it comes to frank talking about death. If he or she isn't willing to follow up hints, there is little that can be done to initiate an open discussion. Research has shown that in fact the dying are most often aware of their true condition – you know for yourself that your body generally tells the truth about your state, and feeling so weak and ill can be ample evidence for many sick people. But everyone has the right to limit how much he admits, even to himself. And while *we* might agree that it is better to be open, it does depend greatly on your individual relationship with your mother or father. As Guy put it:

> Knowing that my father was dying seemed to give me a kind of secret knowledge against him. It seemed wrong that I should know and that he didn't, because he was my father and fathers ought to be more knowledgeable and more powerful than their sons. They told me they'd tried to tell him but that he didn't want to discuss it. I don't remember what we talked about at visiting time, but I know that death never entered the conversation. He would hardly admit he was ill at all; he died very quietly. I wish we could have shared our knowledge, I don't mean great in-depth talks, but just a word or two.

Accepting that your authority figure is growing weaker is that much more difficult if you're not officially supposed to know, and if your mother isn't willing to know either. Acknowledging the truth can however be unexpectedly liberating, as well as giving real value to the time that is left. Like Guy, Hazel was appalled at the power she felt she was given in knowing of her father's condition. She tried to hide it from herself and him, and, one visiting day, talked for a while about the holiday they would all take when he was better.

14

He heard me out, then said, 'I just feel I won't be there.' That was the closest he came to admitting he was dying but it was enough – the truth really hit me in the eyes, and somehow I'd managed to push it away up until then. I went home and cried and cried, but if I'm honest, I must say that having the pretence destroyed was a kind of relief. After that, visits were much easier, and quieter – sadder, too, but I felt he'd given us permission to be sad.

If you can't be sad at such a time, when can you? But letting out the appropriate feelings isn't always as easy as it might seem: sadness has a hundred inappropriate disguises. In addition, making sure you display the proper feelings in front of your mother is a childhood habit that can be hard to lose. To talk openly about death, to reveal emotion, to break down and weep before your mother, may feel too selfish, too melodramatic and too painful. It's not just that your parent is too close to you; it's the frightening admission that her power is on the wane; your life structure is crumbling.

It can take courage to plunge into such conversations. There are no easy answers to a comment such as, 'I don't feel I'm going to be here much longer and I feel very sad about all the things I didn't do.' How easy just to say, 'Don't say that!' It's up to you and your relationship, of course, but perhaps a mother who starts this type of conversation doesn't want to be rebuffed with simplicities. In fact, research has proved that parents are more likely to be hurt by a conspiracy of silence and that you may be able to help if you are willing to listen and talk frankly.

You could also ask if there's anything she wants done after death, such as writing a letter to a long-lost relative, disposing of clothes in a certain way, or making contributions to some charity. Settling such things can be helpful for both sides in accepting what is going on.

What if your parent doesn't unburden herself? Can you or should you intrude? Again, one hint or question is enough. If your mother doesn't 'hear' or changes the subject, you have done your best and all you can do is accept that she doesn't want to talk. Some people value their privacy to the end and feel stronger alone.

Personality changes in your parent

Sorting out your relationship with your dying parent is also likely to be complicated by other factors. First, for some of the time at least, you may not be seeing your mother in her familiar setting but in a hospital ward – with all the paraphernalia of charts, drips and visiting hours.

Then there are the unaccustomed emotions of other family members, which can also make it difficult to be as simple and natural with your dying parent as you might like. Last, but not least, are the effects of any illness. Pain, drugs and the knowledge of oncoming death may all alter your mother's personality, sometimes leading to uncharacteristic and disturbing manifestations of irrationality and negativity.

> Anita had always confided in her mother Yvonne and regarded her as a source of strength in the many emotional turmoils she experienced while growing up. In Anita's mid-20s, Yvonne developed a tumour in the brain which made her increasingly confused and dependent on her daughter. Anita was bewildered by the personality changes in her mother, who became irritable and depressed. Yvonne found fault constantly with Anita for doing little things wrong, such as giving her too large a plate of food, and too often exhausted herself by shouting at her daughter. Anita often felt that her mother had already died and she was caring for a stranger inhabiting her shell.

It is hard to deal with anger and bitterness from a much-loved father or mother – to see your parent degenerate in any way. Memory loss is a poignant example of this – while your consciousness is being sharpened, that of your mother is being diminished. As memories grow more precious to you, they fall further and further out of existence for her. Perhaps the hardest aspect of this kind of mental deterioration, which is one feature of Alzheimer's disease, is to be constantly giving without ever getting much in return. It wears down the most constant goodwill to have your little attentions forgotten as soon as they've been performed, to realize that you and your mother are living on different time scales. Perhaps she's reverted to a time in the past, or perhaps she has lost the concepts of past and future altogether, living only in the present – something which is hard to imagine until you're faced with it and a constant source of stress when you are.

Dealing with constant petty irritation is one thing; handling more dramatic manifestations of degeneration is another. You may not always be able to cope with tearful, angry outbursts as calmly as you'd like, or to soothe continued restlessness from your sick mother. This is where it is important to get as much outside help as possible – you could find a support group which caters particularly for your parent's condition (see Useful addresses at the end of the book).

It can help to realize that, apart from the actual effects of illness or medication, certain emotions are a natural part of dying. Medical observations of dying people have detailed five psychological stages normally experienced – denial and isolation, anger, bargaining ('Please let me live until my son gets married and I'll behave very well/give some money to the hospital chapel'), depression and acceptance. (The bereaved go through a similar process which will be discussed more fully in Chapter 5.) While this may make rather too tidy reading for those experiencing the actual event, it can be reassuring to know that certain emotional changes are the norm – also that they may not come in the form you expected. If you anticipated loving scenes with your dying parent, it can be cruelly disconcerting when, like Anita, you meet with irritation over trivia instead. Do try and accept that changes in your parent have little to do with you personally, and also that she has to come to terms with death in her own way.

Some people feel they can handle anything so long as their mother's basic personality remains unchanged, and very often it is extraordinary how much courage and sense of humour can be displayed by a dying person. You may be amazed at how much people remain themselves. Nevertheless, many have in the end to face a growing absence of personality, or at least the personality you have known. Your parent is likely to seem increasingly remote as he or she moves further and further away from everyday life. Many people have shared Anita's feeling that, as death approaches, the soul has already flown even if the body remains. This, though sometimes uncanny to go through, can take some of the drama and fear from the actual moment of death, which is then experienced as a natural and peaceful ending.

'Unfinished business' with your parent

'Unfinished business' is one of those semi-technical terms which you may come across in books on bereavement and among bereavement counsellors. It can be defined as 'any difficulties in your relationship with your parent which need to be resolved before death'; or just 'anything you feel needs to be said or sorted out'. When tackling this, it is important to bear in mind that, with or without beliefs in an afterlife, death does not have to end a relationship. Parental relationships have a way of influencing lives for many years, perhaps for ever, whether death has intervened or not. Taking this longer view can be helpful because you may not be able to finish all the 'business' right now; you may need more time in which to formulate a different perspective, or in which to garner the life experience which will enable you to understand your parent and yourself better. Alternatively, the relationship with your parents may be such that you know you never would be able to take matters any further no matter what.

Stephen, a 43-year-old writer, felt that any business between him and his parents would never have been finished no matter how much time had been available because both he and they were set in a certain, limited pattern of communication.

Again, 'unfinished business' may not be anything clear, like formal apologies for not becoming a barrister as your parent wished, or for dropping the family religion. There may indeed be issues to be discussed and amends to be made. But, don't look on what you and your parent say before death as necessarily summing everything up. The words of the dying are traditionally deemed to have special meaning – and deep personal value – but they are not the end of the story, and indeed may be out of place.

Moira, a 25-year-old nursery school teacher, found herself taking an increasing share in her mother's physical care while Susan was at home – combing and cutting her hair, helping her with her colostomy bag, washing her soiled nightdresses. Moira felt this was a natural process in which she was in some small measure repaying her mother for all the care that she had taken of her as a child, and without too many words, Moira and her mother reached a conclusion of their living relationship before the final admission to hospital.

This is less easy if your relationship with your parent has been troubled; hangovers from childhood achieve their greatest strength now.

Michael's father, Tom, a difficult man, had had a convoluted, bitter relationship with the family, especially after a family wedding where he had got drunk and caused a scene. The family, already inclined to split into two camps, had maintained the feud ever since. Because of this, Michael was naturally the more upset at his father's dying. Also, as youngest son, Michael felt he had always had to jostle for his father's recognition, and had never quite had it, although he also felt that he of all the family was most supportive of his father, and most like him in character.

What can you do? As Michael discovered, impending death does not necessarily open everyone's eyes and make smooth all the family problems; you cannot shake an obstinate, old father into a recognition of the error of his (and other people's) ways.

The childish need to challenge recognition out of your father or mother is an attempt to control what death is showing cannot be controlled. 'Letting go' of your parent can help: with all her wilful habits of misunderstanding, and all the disastrous 'inner scripts' that may have dominated her life. This may also involve letting go of a picture of your mother – not as she is, but as you would like her to be: more mature, more humane, more able to empathize with you. Disturbing as it may seem to the adult part of ourselves, since our parents may have done much for us, we have to face the fact that our childish inner centre can always demand more.

Paradoxically, there is more of a temptation to idealize an awkward parent after death – to say he was misunderstood and thwarted, or not given enough recognition by the rest of the family. It is possible to guard against this by at least recognizing the truth of your relationship as it stands. You may not be able to do more for now: sometimes, just leaving the business unfinished can be the best way of resolving it. Later, when the worst of grief is over and you feel stronger, you may be able to look at the relationship again.

Role reversal

One of the most painful changes when a parent is dying is starting to reverse your ideas about her strength and capability. It involves coming to terms with the way illness has invaded your mother's privacy, and the way she has become weak and fallible. It can be hard for both sides to adapt to role reversal, with you as the caretaker for at least some of the time.

In fact, role reversal occurs in the normal course of events: as your parents grow older, you often have to take more of *their* care upon yourself. This reversal is however often speedier and so more noticeable if your parent is dying of a terminal illness; within months or even weeks, your help may change from helping your still-mobile father out of the car, to feeding a bedridden invalid with a spoon.

Role reversal can be especially difficult to accept if it interrupts your own emotional dependence on either of your parents.

Although Moira and Anita were both in their mid-20s when they lost their mothers, Anita felt far more vulnerable. She felt that she was an immature 25, and that her mother was being taken from her at a key point in her life. She had just returned from a year's travelling in Australia and India, and felt she needed her mother to talk to as it was time to make some mature choices in life. As a nursery school teacher of some years' standing, Moira at 25 was much more personally established; she was also engaged. When the two girls met and developed a kind of friendship at the hospital, Anita felt bitter that Moira had a fiancé to support her through her mother's loss while she was to all intents and purposes alone.

It is extremely easy to fall into self-pity at some point as your parent slips away. Even if you don't feel like a needy child inside, you may well feel that your parent is too young to die. With the longer life expectancy of today, death at 60 or even 70 can seem like a cheat – Michael, who lost his father at 72, certainly felt the old man could have enjoyed 'a few years more'.

Other relationship changes

The other great change that takes place is with your living parent, who is likely to be more unhappy than you have ever seen him or her. Because of this, you may come in for an unfair share of irritation just because you are in the vicinity. You may be the recipient of emotional scenes or fraught silences, both of which are distressing and draining. What can you do? The feeling of being powerless is very hard, but it may be a reality that for now you cannot always comfort your living parent as you would like. He or she may express appreciation of your presence and efforts one day, only to appear cold or cross the next. Just as with your dying parent, you have to learn to let go of someone whom you may increasingly be unable to reach; also, to accept some more role reversal – for example, looking after someone who does not care whether he is looked after or not. Chapter 8 is devoted to you and your other, living parent but for a start the best thing to do is to forget family roles as far as possible and look at yourselves as individuals struggling against the same blow.

With such a major event at the centre of your life, it would be surprising if your other relationships did not also suffer some changes – your friends, your work colleagues and your neighbours can all seem remote and/or insensitive. Impending bereavement and after death are times when you are likely to feel cut off from the mainstream of life, especially if you do find yourself very caught up with your family.

Unfortunately, you may well experience a genuine lack of empathy from peers, acquaintances and work colleagues. As has been stated before, losing a parent is such a common life event that, while people may express initial sympathy, they may quickly forget your probable feelings as time goes by – after all, death is highly forgettable. Few want to hear or talk about it. It is much easier if you can accept this, turning to genuine friends or bereavement groups for support. This won't be for ever – the friends you feel you can't talk to may still have a future part to play in your life, even if you find you have to put the friendship on hold for now. It can also be helpful not to invest the close people in your life with too much importance, if you can help it. This is partly because this too changes – closeness comes and goes in friendships according to circumstances. Someone you could pour your heart out to may be invaluable now, and a treasured friend for life, but not someone you'll feel the same need to talk to a year or so hence. Your emotions of this period, although perhaps all-consuming for now, are not going to be typical of the rest of your life.

If you have a family of your own, or a long-term partner, these can provide very welcome support – often just by being there.

Michael's wife Joan knew there was little she could do to help him while his father was dying, but she also knew that it would have been much harder for him had he had to go through it alone. Joan's role varied from receiving phone calls in the small hours from Michael in the hospital, to ringing in herself to cheer the family with the news that she had passed her driving test!

Hazel's boyfriend Will would often cook a meal for Hazel and her mother Barbara when they came back at night from their hospital visits, and he also insisted on taking Hazel away for the weekend a few times.

Sharing care – relationships with siblings

Family funerals are notorious for disputes, but trouble can be brewing well before that point. Another feature of parental death is the way in which it traps you within the family, almost in an enforced return to childhood, especially if you have been away making your own life. No matter how much of an adult you may be outside the home, it is difficult to avoid some childhood habits or feelings creeping back when you go home anyway, never mind in a case of serious illness. With the established balance of the family upset by the imminent death of a father or mother, everyone feels insecure and unsure of his or her role.

Guy felt very unsure of what he was supposed to do in the short time he was around his dying father. 'Looking back, I think we were all too young to deal with it – neither my two sisters (19 and 23 at the time) nor myself had a clue. We just brought flowers and kept quiet, really.'

Michael's family had to visit his father Tom in two separate groups as a result of the quarrel which had divided the family some years earlier. Michael was deeply upset that the family was wrangling over his father's deathbed. 'I felt Dad was crying out for love – what really caused me the deepest pain was the fact that one of my brothers just didn't seem to care. He'd be reading the paper over Dad's head or looking at his watch.'

It's true that some people are better at sickbeds than others. But, this is a time when such irritations can really grate, especially in this kind of situation where family discord makes members all the more ready to see the worst side of each other. Even without big complications, it is common to feel, for example, that you are doing more than other family members who are insensitive and neglectful towards the dying parent; or that your motives are purer than theirs in giving your time and attention. This kind of jealous quarrelling for the dying parent's attention is natural. To feel special to the dying parent is a profound need, even if you can manage to be more objective intellectually.

> Anita used to feel, secretly, that only she brought the right kind of flowers to her mother in hospital, though she recognized this as a logic of the emotions rather than of the head. She felt she was on surer ground in her resentment at her brother Louis for constantly sitting at her mother's bedside and trying to 'cheer her up' with jokes and chatter which Anita felt to be both inappropriate and tiring for her mother.

It is common for one child to be the 'coper' of the family – quite often the eldest. This is the one who shops, cooks, and makes sure that Mum or Dad takes the right medicine. The eldest of three, Anita, who returned home for a while, easily fell into the role, but increasingly realized that she would have to share this status with her sister, Karen. Both women felt this would be much easier without the well-meant interference of their brother. Indeed, once he had been forced by business pressure to return to his home in Canada, Anita and Karen established a much easier equilibrium, taking it in turns to share their mother's care until her death.

Having 'something to do' helps to dissipate the frustration of this period. Perhaps it is possible to work out a share of duties with the rest of the family – to have a definite rota for visiting, for example, or to keep an eye on your parent's house, cancel the milk, water the plants, walk the dog, and so on. Sharing duties avoids one person trying to take everything on his or her shoulders. If there have been family feuds, you could agree to differ with your brothers and sisters on other matters, but to form a temporary truce, to work together to deal with the most important thing, your parent's death. You might find it helpful to see your family socially, especially if you don't normally do so – alternatively perhaps close friends or husbands and wives could be asked to step in and provide some emotional coolness if tempers are becoming heated. Otherwise, hard though it might be, it can be more than helpful to detach yourself emotionally from the family circle and just let others be the way they are, recognizing that you will probably not be able to change them!

This is certainly one of the most destabilizing times a family can go through. Decisions have to be made, unaccustomed emotions have to be dealt with, and siblings whom you may not have seen for years have to be met on new, vulnerable ground.

Using the time left

A parent's dying can seem to be made up of petty irritations and major heartache. This is when you need to step back from the pressure of everyday life, and the inevitability of death, to take a more consoling overview of the situation.

No one wants to feel that their mother's life has no further value once the death sentence has been given. Even if your mother is weary of life, and even if death comes as a relief, this final illness by no means invalidates the life which has gone before. Dying people can lead full lives, using the time to travel, take up hobbies or fulfil lifelong ambitions. Even when major activity is no longer possible, it is important to remember that your parent is still living in every sense of the word.

> Hazel would bring soft clay into hospital for her father to model tiny animals with when he was strong enough, and would take them home to bake and paint herself. While he was still at home, Michael's father appreciated the roast chicken and individual fruit crumbles sent over by Michael's wife. Moira would go out and get her mother and herself an ice cream each, or a new book to read. Moira's mother also liked her daughter to help her with her make-up before the doctor's visit, saying that it would be the doctor who died of fright if he saw her without it!

To be labelled 'dying' is the major blow to a person's identity, so it can also be helpful to your parent if you allow her to give to you, as well as rushing to give to her. This was one of the things Anita came to realize in her not very restful relationship with her mother.

> She needed to know that she was still useful to me – that she still mattered. She wanted to make sure I would choose the right career and the right man – even though she did become quite bad-tempered and we never really discussed things properly, I could understand that part of her fussing was that she hated losing control, going when we both felt I still needed her.

Anita's mother wanted to give advice but didn't quite know how or in what form to give it. Anita understood that this was her way of showing care. Because we tend to think in terms of what we can do for the dying, we can forget this need for dying parents to give care to those around, to make sure they leave their children as well provided-for as possible emotionally. It is after all in the nature of a parent to go on being concerned for children, even once they are adults.

Incidentally, someone who is given a 'death sentence' may in fact have a few years yet to live, and may well intend to make the most of them before becoming bedridden. This was the case with Moira's mother.

Moira's mother, Susan, who had always been an energetic soul, had several remissions in what had been diagnosed as terminal cancer. When she was well, she was as much her old self as possible, going out, visiting people, handing out birthday and Christmas cards, and deaf to all suggestions that she should rest or take it a bit easier. Moira, at first inclined to be resentful at the way her mother spread herself around, was later able to see this as the need of a dying person to give.

This may be a time when giving and care on both sides can be appreciated at its purest, without being clouded by the usual distractions of work, money and so on.

The curtailing of time is one of the hardest things to accept about this period; life has suddenly shrunk to a few months, a few weeks, and it may be necessary to define living in terms of being rather than doing. Just to have your parent being him or herself – bossy, humorous, cranky, opinionated – can however be immensely reassuring. Taken day by day, life can still yield meaning, richness and peace, even in small doses.

Initiating the grieving process

Grief will have its way: for our future well-being, it must come out. While there is life, there may be hope – that is, grieving can sometimes be deferred. But, there are all sorts of little griefs before the day of the big one – for example, the grief that comes when your parent becomes too weak to travel by train, too weak to drive, too weak to shake a pillow; or when she loses interest in matters which used to concern her or you so closely, such as your own family life or that of your siblings.

The suspense of this pre-death period can often cause a kind of numbness. You carry on as best you can, without letting too many emotions impede you, perhaps waiting for the right moment to let go and to start feeling your grief. And perhaps you feel that the right moment isn't until after death, that you'll let it all out then. For now, you may well feel that you need to stay numb in order to cope. But, it is worth saying that the grieving process can and does start before death.

But, if you can't grieve to order, grief is not something that you let out so as to feel healthy again. It isn't a case of saying that the sooner you begin to grieve, the sooner it will be over and the better for you. Grief is not a condition which you 'get over' like an illness, but a life experience; it demands a long-term response and cannot be hurried through or swept away. This is the sense in which grief can be said to be positive; there is no substitute for experience when it comes to forging new skills and new strengths with which to face the rest of your life.

Meanwhile, it may well be that you can begin to grieve before your parent dies, especially if she is ill for months or even years beforehand. Grief stops and starts for a long time before it is really absorbed, however: by the time you feel you can resume your life without a huge burden of sorrow, you will have become a rather different person. You will be someone who has been changed at depth by the grief you have lived through.

But this is to look ahead. Meanwhile, to sum up, it's a time when your closest relationships will be called upon to provide support in a way which was never dreamed of beforehand. You need to find a balance between looking after yourself, looking after others, and finding some sort of outside support. It's a time when emotions are likely to be much more rough and raw than the gentle deathbed scenarios you may have pictured. To get through this period more easily, you may need to suspend judgement, especially where friendships are concerned. Last, but not least, you can also help yourself by holding on to the knowledge that the bedrock of your identity is there, even if it feels confused or non-existent in the upheaval caused by your mother or father's death.

3

When death comes

No matter what emotional preparations we have made for death, it is very hard to accept when it actually does take place, because our sense of reality is shaken so deeply. It is surprising how much we need our day-to-day routine to feel anchored; small changes can put us out, like having our desk moved at work or being distracted by toothache. Now, with the normal routine suspended so totally, with the unthinkable actually happening, our minds may be unable to take it in. The lead up to death, the event itself and the time just afterwards, touch us too closely to be viewed within the normal parameters of life. Like it or not, we are cut off from the busy humdrum of the ordinary day; like war, death cuts through all ordinary conditions. This experience will eventually be assimilated into the fabric of your life; normality will return, new beginnings will be made, you will discover unsuspected sources of strength and maturity within yourself, painful though the process will be. Also, you will forge new bonds with other people – not immediately, when you feel that no one can understand or enter into your grief, but in the long term. There is a temptation after such a close death to divide people mentally into insiders (those who have also suffered) and outsiders (those still living in ignorance of what death really means). When this mellows with time, it can leave you with a valuable extra sensitivity towards other people. Finally, you may well feel stronger for having had to confront some of life's deepest questions, to have looked death in the face and perhaps formulated your own concept of it to sustain you through life.

All this is in the future, outside the immediate context of your parent dying – but try and hang on to the idea, however remote it seems, that there is indeed a future, more varied and enriching than can be imagined in the desolate circumstances of the present.

Last visits: waiting for death

There are few things more harrowing than the weeks and days just before death. It's the not knowing exactly when death will take place – the wondering as you mount the hospital steps how your father will be today, how much further he may have slipped away, whether he will die while you're there, and if so, how on earth you will be able to bear it. It's a time of great confusion, when a day can feel like a week, and a week like a year. If death is protracted, it may also be a time when your emotions switch off. After going in expecting yet another night to be the last, attending your father's deathbed becomes a matter of sheer physical endurance.

> The doctors told Michael that his father was dying, but it was about three weeks before this actually happened. During most of this time, Tom was unconscious, his wasted body looking as like death as made no difference, so that the family couldn't understand how Tom could keep going. Michael, who expected every day to be the last, wanted to spend as much time with his dad as possible, especially as he knew Tom hadn't wanted to be alone while conscious. But with this gruelling visiting routine, which meant sitting up to the small hours every day, Michael became absolutely exhausted. His own family suffered too – his wife would wait up for him, or for his phone calls from the hospital, she too expecting every call to deliver the awaited news.

The dying person's need to grieve

> Anita's mother slipped into unconsciousness during her last week of life, but Anita was horrified to notice her weeping in her sleep at intervals – 'crying for her life', as an old Irish nurse put it.

The dying person does need to 'cry for his life' – to mourn the mistakes, the missed opportunities and the less-than-perfect relationships; to mourn above all the simple fact that time is running out and that there will be no further chances to do more or to put things right. Going through this grief can help a dying person come to terms with the unsatisfactory elements in his life so, although bitterly upsetting to see, it can be viewed as a painful route towards peace.

Like all mourning, the grief of the dying is to some extent a private process. This is partly what makes it so painful to see: the stony face, the numbed self-absorption in your father or mother which shuts you out. Sometimes there is little you can do but let him go through it; you cannot but help share his pain, but it can seem as if this sharing does not penetrate through to your father. Nevertheless, the very sick do often want company even if they aren't up to talking: you can help just by being there.

Also, you may be able to help in other ways – if your father gives you an opening and starts to talk about his feelings. This is no longer a question of talking about the fact that he is dying, or of asking if there is anything he wants done after death, or of checking out any private fears he may have, as was discussed in Chapter 2: it is just acknowledging your father's feelings of grief at losing his life. These conversations can be very simple; if your father says he's depressed, for example, all you can really say is words to the effect of 'I'm very sorry to hear that', because once you've spoken the bare truth, what more is there to say? You cannot console him with facile comments to the effect that he'll be better soon.

But, neither do you need to make it more painful with too many naked emotions, or by pushing him further to talk. By now you may feel you've been through all the emotions anyway, and are squeezed dry; it may be almost as much of an effort for you to talk as for your father. Try and follow where he leads. He may simply want you to be around: being shut alone with his grief can be just as isolating for your dying father as for you.

Even if your parent is in a coma, like Anita's mother, he may still be conscious to some degree of what is going on around him. It is quite common for a previously unconscious person suddenly to wake up and be able to repeat conversations that have been going on around his bedside. Holding your father's hand, and giving simple words of reassurance and love is not a waste of energy. As death comes closer, the hearing is the last sense of the dying person to go.

Letting go

There comes a moment when our parent needs to die, and we need to let go. But, what is letting go, exactly? By no means is it a decision not to think about your parent any more, to assume indifference, or to switch off emotionally. One way of defining it is as a 'deep acceptance of our lack of power in the face of death'. This is something we all know we ought to have: but actually having it is well-nigh impossible unless death itself forces it upon us. Who wants to 'let go' of their mother behind the drawn curtains of a bed in a public ward? Who feels they *can* let go after a 2 a.m. phone call from the ward sister to say that their father has finally died?

Anita could not accept her mother's final submission. It seemed so strange in someone who had always been a fighting spirit. It took Anita a long time before she was able to accept that her mother may have made important inner changes during her last week or so of coma.

It is worth noting that Anita's difficulty in letting go was compounded by the troubles she had always had in her relationship with her mother – at a fundamental level, it just didn't seem right that she was no longer there to quarrel with!

It can be a very fine line between caring for your dying parent, an activity which belongs to life, and accepting his gradual departure. The death process itself does often help – as the dying person becomes more remote, so it becomes easier to let go. But there is still plenty of room for the protest which makes up so much of grief.

Being present at death

Many people find that witnessing death is far worse in anticipation than in reality. Even if the lead up to death is harrowing, death itself is often a peaceful moment, as Hazel found.

> It was all very calm – after all, we knew it was going to happen, we'd been prepared for it for some months now. It was like something that just had to be. And it was nice because we were all there.

It's the terrible days and hours beforehand that can be so traumatic, with your father wired up to machines in intensive care or in a geriatric ward, made all but unrecognizable by illness, when medical treatment may make you feel your parent has lost all right to die with dignity.

In the last few hours, you are likely to see increased physical changes. The face may seem to fall in, becoming more skeletal; breathing is more irregular and hoarser. Often, staff will give a drug to dry up the secretions in the throat which, though painless to the patient, can be so distressing to listen to.

Often the last breath is especially deep – a kind of long sigh, and life departs. This is the physical sum of it.

But, as one hospital chaplain pointed out, people have a habit of dying much as they have lived. They may keep a family dancing round the bedside as they kept it dancing around them in life; they may hang on for days and days and then finally die when everyone's out of the room; they may be quiet and unobtrusive, as if they didn't want to be a bother.

In some cases, you might want to do a little more than view the dead body – Michael combed his father's hair for him, Anita put her mother's engagement ring on her finger as her father wanted her to be buried with it. One woman, a nurse, helped to lay her mother out as a last act of love – although another nurse who lost her mother refused when asked if she would like to do the same. It is up to you how much you choose to do.

Just afterwards

No matter what emotional preparations we may have made for impending death, it is very hard to take in when it actually happens. This tends to mark the real beginning of our questioning the nature of death. Where has that person gone? It may not even be a matter of considering something potentially huge, like the soul; it is difficult to think about something so abstract, but we may find ourselves wondering about details. What has become of all the little idiosyncracies, such as a certain way of knotting a tie, always humming the same song or persistently leaving the cutlery drawer open? It is too much for the human mind to cope with: yet, in the immediate aftermath of death we may find ourselves probing further and further into the unknown, trying to see where our parent has gone, trying to follow as far as we can go. This is partly why one feels so isolated in immediate bereavement.

It's a time of extreme fragility, when the least word can set off pain. Many people have reported how tender and bruised they felt in the first few weeks.

> Guy felt that the least word grated; he couldn't bear to listen to the news in case there was any mention of hospitals or death, and he couldn't drive past the hospital where his father had died. These feelings faded gradually over the next 18 months.

Alternatively, you may not feel what you consider to be the appropriate emotions. Tears may not come, you may feel not sorrow but, for example, extreme fatigue at the strain of death. The period just after a death can be a time of immense relief, a time to let all the exhaustion out, especially if you have been involved in a lengthy dying process. Michael's night visits to the hospital really caught up with him once Tom had finally died; Moira was another person who realized how much her stamina had been depleted in her mother's last days.

> It sounds awful, but I remember I just stayed in bed for the whole of the next day after Mum died, and got my sister to bring me up breakfast. I felt so shattered – as if I'd been hit over the head with a sandbag, drained in every way. I wanted someone to do a bit of looking after me – I felt I'd been giving out so much. I just couldn't make any more efforts at all.

This feeling of extreme fatigue may last for some weeks, and to refer back to Chapter 1, this is a time when you do need to take care of yourself. If you are staying with or live close to family, perhaps you could take it in turns to look after each other for a while. Or it might be an idea to go and stay with a close friend who will tuck you up with cocoa and arrange the reclining chairs in the sunlounge, but who doesn't mind accommodating you when you want to be alone. Of course you have duties of your own, and may have to struggle on with a tiring job or caring for children, but within the context of these duties looking after yourself should be a priority.

The impact on your own family

If you have a family of your own, the comfort can be easier to come by, although this period immediately after death can be an unexpected strain. If your partner has been through it all with you, he or she may feel less sorrow and more relief at the death of someone who after all was not a natural parent, and may want to get on with normal living now.

Michael's wife Joan felt that her abilities as a caretaker had been quite stretched during Tom's illness. She was also fed up with his wrangling family, and wanted Michael to herself again. He, however, would lie in late whenever possible and also sleep a lot during the afternoons at weekends. While Joan understood his exhaustion in one way, in another she did feel rather annoyed at the way in which Tom, who had never taken much notice of her, continued to play an influential part in their lives. The situation was also made worse by the demands of their children, which Michael couldn't always meet.

In other words, families have to be ready to extend their support after death, throughout the period of grief. It is natural to have a little jealousy, but unrealistic to make the normal demands on someone who is stunned and isolated by the impact of death. It's something which can separate the closest couples for a while – equally, the bereaved partner may feel impatience at the one who 'doesn't understand'. It is hard for two people to stand on exactly the same ground when one has lost a parent and the other not, although some people do mourn an in-law's death as if it were their own flesh and blood. However, perhaps this is a time for the more detached partner to take on the leading role, to assume more responsibilities, until her spouse has regained the balance lost in his immediate grief.

4

Sudden death

Although many people lose their parents relatively late in life, through lingering illnesses, some are bereaved without warning. This may be by means of a short illness, or a sudden collapse, with death following minutes or hours later. Sadly, this is not uncommon in a country which still scores high on international tables of heart disease. Apart from the heart attack, there are other illnesses which can cause speedy death, such as a stroke, pneumonia or even a virulent cancer. While we know that an accident is always possible, it is still a terrific shock when one causes death. Violent death (murder and suicide) are less common but sadly have to be considered.

The impact of sudden death is different from the more protracted death, especially at first. Life changes from one minute to the next. There is no time to make preparations, no forewarning (although sometimes in the case of heart attack or other illness there may have been a few signs). It is hard to appreciate the shock of this unless you have been through it – the time needed just to take the news in, the physical sensations of shock (see Chapter 1), the breaking up not just of plans and expectations, but of our whole view of the world. We will never feel the same again about a life in which such things can happen, where the impossible has become fact and *still* can't be understood. It is at this point that we grasp all the difference between knowing that such events do take place, and having one of them strike our own lives. It's a difference which seems to pose an irreconcilable gap between the way we were experiencing life beforehand, and the way we experience it afterwards.

Eventually, the event becomes part of the pattern of our lives; it becomes a reference point, a time from which we may feel that our present identities have developed. One of the main aspects of any parent's death is the way it forms a 'before and after', with different views and identities belonging to each era. The divide is that much sharper with sudden death.

We do tend to have a mental picture of our parents living rosily in retirement and fading peacefully away at the very end of busy, useful lives. When this is truncated by sudden or violent death, bereavement is that much more difficult, both for you and for your other parent, who may need more of your support than if the death had been gradual and expected.

Apart from the fact that the shock is worse, mourning may be more complicated and longer. There may especially be more work to do in the initial period of grief. It is often more difficult to find some eventual meaning in what has happened. There can be a temptation to blame your dead father or mother for the way in which they met their fate. It is also not uncommon for a person who has died suddenly or violently to become idealized. When you hear the news of sudden death, you can understand where the expression, 'It's a blow', came from. News of this kind *is* a physical blow – you may feel as if you've actually been hit in the body, the air knocked out of you. To be told that your mother is dying is bad enough (as discussed in Chapter 1), but it's true that while there is life there is hope. It isn't the same as being told that she is actually dead.

Shock can last several days after sudden death, and its effects must not be under-estimated. Again, look after yourself – keep warm and drink plenty of (non-alcoholic) fluids even if you can't eat. You may feel numbed, suspended from normal life – a reaction which can actually be protective, giving you time to accustom yourself to the news before you start experiencing any of the feelings connected with it.

Once you do start feeling, the anger may be greater than if your parent had died gradually – it is often easier to direct it. If for example your father or mother died in a road accident, the other driver or drivers involved can become a focus for anger. This is especially true following large-scale disasters, including terrorist attack. Research has suggested that it can actually be healthier if relatives of those killed are able to direct their anger (i.e. pressing for criminal charges to be carried out against those seen as responsible, or campaigning for better safety precautions).

Sudden death is more often heard about than witnessed. Because of this, there may be a particular anguish in wondering what your father or mother's last moments were like: terrified, pain-filled? It is natural to let his or her seconds or minutes of dying become your hours and hours of emotional distress. It may not be possible to switch off your thoughts by mental discipline alone, so at some stage you may well need to talk to someone (see 'Interrupted relationships' below, and Chapter 9).

The fact that you 'weren't there' can also be a source of long-lasting regret – or that there may not have been anyone there. You may also have to deal with the lengthy, painful mental process of 'if only'. If only your father had taken a later train, if only your mother had consulted a doctor earlier, and so on. Finally, sudden deaths are often bizarre, like nightmares, because they are so very unexpected, especially if they are accidents.

> Peter's father died hours after a cricket ball hit him on the bridge of the nose; Glen's father died a few days after being crushed in a crowd at Trafalgar Square one New Year's Eve; Ruth's mother died after being hit by a skip which a lorry was unloading.

Adapting the strangeness of some events to the everyday world in which we may have lived so far, and to a faith if we have one, must be one of the most daunting of all life experiences. It's probably more accurate to say that adaptation of this kind isn't really possible. Sudden death, more than any other kind, may force us to re-examine our values and the way we live our lives.

Sudden illness

Many people know someone who's died of a stroke or heart attack – the latter is the most common form of sudden death from natural causes in this country. However, a heart attack doesn't always come totally without warning. There may have been a period of ill-health, some ominous symptoms, or even another attack earlier on. Even so, the death itself is often very sudden.

> Colin, a 53-year-old actor, knew his father had endured one heart attack some years previously. His father's health had been mediocre ever since. But, when Joe died at 79 of another attack, it was still a shock as the death itself was very sudden – Colin's mother found Joe sitting dead in front of the television one afternoon.

In this kind of situation, there may also be a kind of helpless anger at your parent if you feel he could somehow have avoided the death. This is not always related to the facts: Colin certainly felt that Joe was to blame for not looking after himself better, although in fact Joe had modified his lifestyle quite a lot after his first illness.

There may also be a feeling of your parent having been 'cut off in his prime', especially if (as often happens) a heart attack causes death at a rather earlier age than might have been anticipated. Another feature of the heart attack or stroke can be the lack of dignity with which it brings death. It is distressing to live with the mental image of a father fallen to the pavement and unable to rise, or found dead half-dressed. The pathos and awkwardness of this kind of death are things which need to be worked through in grief, although in the long term they should not be allowed to colour your view of your parent's whole life. If your father or mother dies after a short illness, you are likely to go through similar shock, but, sadly, preceded by a few harrowing days. We are so accustomed to the rescues performed by modern medicine that we're often not prepared for it to fail.

> Doreen's elderly mother, who actually had a weak heart, was admitted to intensive care with severe gastro-enteritis. Despite the best efforts of the staff, she died three days later.

In this case, the urge to blame the medical staff can be even stronger than with a terminal illness, although in fact Doreen had nothing but praise for the efforts of her local hospital. There's also the feeling that surely you could have stepped in with preventative measures earlier on. Doreen says:

> I felt, surely there must have been something I could have done – you know, called in on her a day or two earlier, made her a cup of tea – she got very dehydrated. And I was bitterly cross with her for not picking up the phone and telling me she didn't feel well until it was too late. That old thing of not wanting to be a bother.

Any illness in a parent can easily be felt as a reproach – we may feel that it happened because we haven't been keeping an eye on his welfare, and may long for a chance to put this right when he's well again. When the event defies our expectations, it may need a great deal of time and reassurance before this guilt subsides. In this case, it is worth talking to the medical staff who attended your parent, to satisfy yourself that everything possible was done. You could also ask other family members and friends to give a more objective appraisal of how much you did for your parent, and perhaps to remind you that for other people there is only so much that can ever be done.

Accident

Some people feel that an accident does often at least have the merit of being 'a quick way to go', although not if you yourself feel you might prefer to know that you were dying so that you could prepare yourself. However, it can certainly be consoling if your father or mother died at once or soon after an accident, with just a short time of pain.

What isn't easy to overcome is the force of your own mental and emotional protest. Ruth, a 38-year-old health visitor, was called home from work one afternoon with the news that her mother was dead.

That night, I kept thinking that I must ring and tell her the news. I just couldn't take in that she wouldn't be there – I always went to her with anything important. This happened again and again during the night – I was dozing on and off, I couldn't sleep, and I kept thinking that I had to ring my mother, there was something very important to tell her. Every so often I'd wake up fully and realize that this was a true-life nightmare, that if you believe in hell, this was it. I had no sense of time – I felt that I would never come out of this, that this was the end for me, too.

This mental work is extraordinarily exhausting; you may find that, out of habit, the mind casts round for some relief or distraction so that it is falling back on the news continuously. The shock doesn't come once, but hundreds of times. You may also need to replay the details of the accident in your mind again and again, not just at first, but for months to come. Anger can be especially virulent after an accident. The apparent senselessness of it, the fact that it might have been avoided, can very easily release the instinct to blame mentioned above.

Ruth couldn't forgive the lorry driver who'd been handling the unloading of the skip. Although the driver had been overwhelmed with distress himself, Ruth felt that he was no better than a murderer. She couldn't bring herself to believe that it was just an accident, feeling that there must have been some intention, some volition.

There is the temptation to blame our parent – just as with a heart attack or other illness, it is common to feel that with a little more care the accident could have been avoided – even that our parent was foolishly courting death by, say, riding a bike on busy roads, or, in Ruth's mother's case, waiting to cross the road just by the lorry. This is usually unfounded, although occasionally there can be more of a link between lifestyle and death – for example, one woman's mother, a heavy and habitual drinker, fell down the stairs when drunk, breaking her neck. Generally, though, this 'if only' type of thinking has a limited relation to the reality of the event. It needs a great deal of working through before the accident can be accepted as it happened. Since accidents threaten everybody's safety ('It could happen to me'), the need to find someone to blame is that much stronger.

Murder

Susan's father died in a stabbing incident in the street – one of those senseless, one-in-a-thousand chances. For many months afterwards she imagined what had happened, running through what must have happened in several different ways. 'I felt so utterly desolate that he'd died in that way alone – that there hadn't been anyone there to help him.'

The utter solitude of murder is very hard to bear, and so is the appalling degradation. The father or mother who was once looked up to has become an object of hate of the most vicious and unreasonable kind, and one whose result can't be undone. Murder of a parent can be particularly frightening if it triggers off any childhood echoes of wanting to kill him or her yourself. What angry child doesn't at some point threaten a parent with death, either aloud or in silence?

Sudden death, such as accident and murder in particular, can provoke the question: 'How could she have let it happen to her? How could the father or mother we knew have allowed such a thing?' It's the feeling that if this could happen, you really didn't know your parent, that he had some ghastly secret up his sleeve which was only revealed by his death. Behind this lurks the old idea that the way we live determines our death; that at some level we all consent to our death, or even choose it.

> Susan was greatly distressed by her suspicions of her murdered father, especially as the murderer was never caught and no motive established for the crime. Had there been some side of his life which the family hadn't known about? Had he been pursuing some private path which had led to his own destruction? 'The police asked us if we knew of anyone who had a vendetta against him – the idea was so foreign to Dad, just so unlike the person we knew. He was the last person to get himself murdered – he was a civilized man – was there something we didn't know about him? I've just had to live with that mystery.'

The idea that the victim on some unknown level acquiesced in his death – that there are oppressors and victims – can be traced back to primitive societies. The idea of karma (the person meeting the experiences he or she needs in order to grow spiritually) also plays a part in such thinking, perhaps a rather guilt-ridden part. Under the influence of the twentieth century's psychological pioneers, such as Freud and Jung, we are also accustomed to thinking of ourselves as having unconscious minds with unconscious purposes.

These are ideas which need careful handling if they are not to add to the anguish felt after sudden or violent death. For a start, they need to be differentiated from, say, the very old lady who quietly waves away food and medicine because 'it's time'. Some people do have an awareness that their time has come. Again, a blatant disregard for health could be viewed with suspicion – the person who refuses to alter a stressful life and poor diet after a heart attack, the one who refuses to give up alcohol when warned of cirrhosis. On some level, and in some circumstances, some people do undoubtedly choose death. But is it fair – let alone true – to accuse someone of a death-wish because his life has ended in tragedy?

Apart from the anger and guilt we feel at our parents for abandoning us in this way, the death-wish idea could also be linked to our view of our parents as powerful – so powerful that only they could decide on their deaths. Perhaps we need to look at how thoroughly such a death destroys any lingering childhood notions of a parent's omniscience. With one part of ourselves, we are unable to believe that he or she didn't have some say in what happened. In the end, however, we do have to respect our parent's privacy. Our control over the form of his or her life and death is strictly limited.

Violent deaths bring a chain of often unforeseen consequences (true of large-scale accidents and disasters as well as murders). For example, you may have to deal with the police. Investigations can last for many months and after some initial contact with the police, you may hear nothing for a long time. Families of those who've lost someone through murder have spoken of the 'double assault' they undergo – not just the violent death of a loved one, but the intrusion of police, coroners and other agents of the law. They may not be able to bury or even see the body; information given can be patchy and irregular, greatly adding to distress. Eventually there may be a trial to be attended, which will naturally re-open all the old wounds. Hatred of the murderer, and the burning desire to bring him or her to justice, can be frighteningly powerful. Publicity can also add to the confusion and distress of this time, and you may have to consider carefully exactly how much you choose to say to the press.

To cope with the additional pressures, it is well worth considering a victim support group or similar (see Chapter 8 or the back of the book). You will gain not merely support but status with which to confront these problems; life will have that much more order and purpose, both of which can be very important when it comes to living through grief.

Suicide

Suicide above all brings long-term feelings of sorrow, anger and guilt. Why didn't he or she come to us with the problem instead of taking this drastic step? Why didn't she come to be looked after for a few days? Did she really see us as useless? Couldn't we have been allowed to mother (or father) her for a change? These feelings of rejection, which exist in any death, are even stronger with suicide. Indeed, it is the anti-social nature of the act which led to suicide being traditionally regarded as taboo. Although suicide may only seem to affect one person, it is often seen as a violence against others, involving them either implic-itly, or explicitly, by means of notes to which there can be no reply. The guilt and remorse which suicide evoke can be violent indeed.

But, the confused feelings of those who die by suicide cannot be taken as making any valid statements as far as those left behind are concerned; psychologists are extremely doubtful as to whether the 'rational suicide' ever exists, believing it more likely that some degree of mental disturbance does usually accompany suicide. This can be particularly hard to take in if, as sometimes happens, the motive for the suicide was apparently altruistic.

> Emily's mother committed suicide after being diagnosed as having advanced ovarian cancer – she was unable to face the prospect of being such a burden on her family. Emily found herself very confused by this – didn't her mother's thinking seem to bear them a reproach? Did she consider the family incapable of going through the forthcoming ordeal? Wasn't it patronizing of her to take matters into her own hands? Or was it a death full of dignity and self-sacrifice?

To all such questions, the family of the suicide is left to find its own answers – if it can. Unfortunately, part of coming to terms with what has happened may be an acceptance that the answers will never truly be known.

One unforeseen difficulty of both murder and suicide can be how to explain the death to others in the future. You may feel it's an uncalled-for burden to put up with the shock or curiosity of others who may not otherwise have been concerned with the death. You may shrink from explaining if someone happens to ask what your mother died of. In this case, to protect yourself, you might want to think of a short answer such as 'In an accident'. Whether you choose to say more can then depend on the nature of the curiosity shown in response, and on your own feelings. You are never obliged to talk for the satisfaction of someone else, be it a friend, a counsellor or therapist, or the press.

Interrupted relationships

One of the features of sudden death is that it allows no time for winding up 'unfinished business' (see Chapter 2). Things you might have said during a terminal illness remain unspoken; the relationship is truncated just as it is.

Glen had had a tiff with his father about an unpaid loan and had been avoiding him for a month while he tried to get the money together. His regret that his father hadn't seen him as more responsible was one of the most persistent features of his grief.

If you have established a more adult, equal relationship with your parent, it can be just as much of a blow to be suddenly deprived of it.

Colin felt it was only since his father's first heart attack that he had really come to know him. Since that illness, Joe, formerly on the irritable side, had mellowed, becoming milder and more open, readier to tell stories of his youth, more interested in Colin's own two children, and generally with more time and chat to spare for people.

At least in terminal illness there is a chance to prepare yourself for the death and to round a relationship off. Coming to terms with the truncating of a relationship is more complex and takes longer; the mind needs to work over all the loose ends, all the regrets, in the period of initial grief, rather than the time leading up to death. It may be more difficult to accept that (as Stephen the writer pointed out in an earlier chapter) sometimes relationships must remain with so much unspoken because of habits of limited communication. This is often part of idealizing the parent who has died suddenly.

Colin was bitterly regretful for all the long talks he and Joe would never have, and would even run imaginary conversations through his head. When he mentioned this to his mother, she thought for a moment and then replied, 'But you just used to watch TV together most of the time!'

Nevertheless, idealizing a relationship, or fixing on to one aspect of it, can be a way of managing your loss, of giving it structure until you feel strong enough to admit the imperfections that used to exist in it.

Some people feel a need to do something more to create this structure, to mark the ending of a relationship and round off the 'unfinished business'.

Ruth was deeply upset that the jumper she had been knitting for her mother would now remain unfinished. She decided to complete it and give it to her aunt, who had been her mother's favourite sister. Glen used the money he owed his father to buy a small second-hand car for his mother, to make her life easier. On the advice of his bereavement support group, Colin tried to write a letter to his father, found he couldn't, and burnt his attempt, feeling that just trying had got something out of his system.

Must it rule your life?

The memories accompanying sudden or violent death are not easy to lose and may haunt us without mercy in the first months and years of bereavement. Nevertheless, at some point it becomes possible not so much to make an effort as to exercise choice in whether we allow these memories to continue to dominate us.

This point may be reached sooner if we have been able to talk regularly to someone, perhaps a bereavement counsellor, perhaps a minister – someone who is prepared to listen but whose friendship you aren't draining by repeated requests for a listener.

Depending on the circumstances of your parent's death, you may well be offered help and counselling (e.g. especially after a large-scale accident or disaster). However, it can be more effective if it is *you* who chooses to seek help; the motivation that comes from within is much more of a propulsion towards health than that which is 'offered' externally. Getting to this point can be difficult and lengthy.

It took Susan two years before she was able to discuss her father's death with anyone. She felt others would have turned away from her in repulsion, that their world just didn't admit such shocking events. Not being a church-goer, she didn't know where to seek the help she knew she needed so badly, and she did feel very isolated during this period. Finally, she read an article about victim support groups in the paper and, realizing that this was what she wanted, managed to contact one.

In the end, the way your father or mother died is not a complete statement about their lives: much more remains to be remembered. To concentrate only on the manner of the end deprives not only *our parents* of their total identity but *us* of a rounder perspective. You could try asking yourself how your parent would like to be thought of: as a person who died dramatically; or as someone who'd led a reasonably full and useful life, with a fair share of irritation, sacrifice, trivia and humour?

5

The abandoned child: grief

Read any book on mourning, and you will see that reactions to any death are well documented, tending to follow a certain course of shock, disbelief, depression, and so on. Reading the list of expected reactions can make you feel as if you are on some conveyor belt of grief, being shuttled along from one emotion to the next – perhaps even feeling that, although your grief is isolating, it isn't very private if other people can label it so conveniently and simply. But, we do all react to grief in different ways. Psychological research, while not always immediately helpful to a bereaved person, can at least give some idea of the range of emotions you may go through, even if (in your case) they don't actually follow the expected 'stages'.

These kinds of feelings can be accentuated by the death of a parent in particular because, to your mother or father, you were always special, even if you weren't making any particular mark in the world. Now that that important person has gone, your grief can't be acknowledged. The person who used to comprehend all your feelings as special has gone. It is this loss of identity which can make you feel that your grief is ordinary, without distinguishing marks.

The feeling of being an 'abandoned child' also gives a rather different focus to the grief which follows the death of a parent – a reaction which can strike at any age. According to one major bereavement support organization, it is by no means uncommon for people of 60 or more to speak of themselves in bewilderment as orphans. Having a parent live until you yourself are advanced in years can leave you arrested at a certain stage of development – you never have to move on from your concept of yourself as someone's child, even if this isn't quite realized until one of your parents dies.

> Colin was a mature 53-year-old when his father died of a heart attack. However, Colin felt he could not do what he most wished – to grieve as a child. He felt he needed permission to feel like a child in an adult society – even to cry aloud. He felt that, with his greying hair and ageing face, he was expected to be adult about it all when in fact he felt the paralysing isolation of a small child lost in a huge supermarket. Colin felt ashamed of the extravagant words he needed to describe his emotions.

Coming to terms with your new identity is a major part of this bereavement – you have to get used to the fact that you are no longer someone's child. For some people, it has to be said that this always remains impossible and they cannot help visualizing themselves as a child of a loving parent still; one who remains concerned about their lives, but from a remote vantage – 'looking down' as it were from some childlike heaven, perhaps influencing their lives for the better in subtle ways. However, in the long term, letting such images fade into the background can constitute a major part of a new maturity. Much as a parent may be loved and depended upon, it is also in the nature of a child to want independence.

The funeral

The funeral is an important part of grieving; not only is it a formal goodbye, it can also mark the point from which you first begin to come to grips with a grief-filled life.

For many, the period between death and the funeral can be the worst part of the whole affair, particularly if death has taken place quite quickly, without that prolonged waiting by your dying parent's bedside.

Stephen's mother was taken into hospital with heart failure and died five hours later. Her death wasn't entirely unexpected, as she'd had cancer, well controlled by drugs, for the past seven years, but Stephen found the few days before the funeral absolutely unbearable. Normal life was totally suspended; it was impossible to do anything except think about death and try and assimilate the loss.

One feature of this time can be having to act parentally, and having to arrange the funeral can to some extent ease the painful vacuum of these few days. Whatever your share in the arrangements, funerals (like deaths) do have a tendency to mirror the character of the dead person: they may be gregarious affairs; or quiet, with few attending.

Guy's father's funeral, for example, was limited to the immediate family and one or two good friends. Guy had always viewed his father as a well-liked man, but this quiet affair made Guy think his father's life had been more constricted than he had ever realized. However, Guy also sympathized with his mother's evident desire to respect his father's privacy in this way. Michael, although he was well aware of his father's difficult personality, was deeply saddened by the fact that no friends attended his father's funeral, and that some family members weren't even speaking to each other. The whole service seemed to underline just how alienated Tom had been, and some of his cantankerous ways seemed to seep through even into the details of the events. For example, Michael and his eldest brother had a row with the vicar before the service as to the exact point at which the coffin should be carried in!

Funeral ovations are often a delicate matter for the person conducting the service, especially if the departed was not a 'model of amiability'. *De mortuis nil nisi . . . ?* To remember without eulogizing, and without giving offence to grieving family members, sometimes needs courage! However, it does bring a certain realistic warmth to the service if character defects can receive their tribute as well as virtues. This can be no more than the briefest of mentions – 'Those of us who were privileged to know George, and at times to bear with him – ' as one vicar put it, a sally which actually drew an appreciative remark from the daughter in question, Jane, as to how he'd 'got Dad to a T!'

> Let's face it, Dad could be a bit of a handful sometimes – snapping at the nurses, finding fault with everything you tried to do for him. He was like a big, grumpy child – you loved him, of course, but he didn't half make you mad! I always saw through him, and the vicar did too, and it was nice not to have to pretend he was a saint just because he'd died.

Otherwise, there can be a kind of emptiness, a cold pretence which doesn't fully acknowledge the deceased, with his human bundle of imperfections.

Sometimes the funeral can be a starting point for wondering how much about your parent's life you really did know. Sometimes old friends may turn up whose existence you never suspected, throwing a totally new light on your parent's personality and past. Old friends who attend the service are not just comforting proof of how much your parent was loved, invaluable though that is. It can also make your identity stronger to see parts of your parent's life filled in by people who can talk to you of times before your birth, or in your earliest years before you can remember. Because you are now the 'culture-carrier', as one bereavement writer has put it, you suddenly have a greater need to know of your family history; you need to know more about what you are carrying. You're in the process of re-evaluating ideas and attitudes to all kinds of subjects – art, religion, commerce, education – and measuring your own stance against that of the family can really help (see Chapter 6).

Also, there's the very natural desire to talk about someone so dear to you, and to hear him or her spoken about – a need which isn't always recognized by people who 'don't know what to say' in the face of bereavement. Sometimes this is less of a barrier with bereaved adult children because of the attitude that the death of a parent is somehow less painful because it must be expected; people might more readily talk to you than to your other parent, to avoid giving him or her pain, though this isn't necessarily so. It is also possible to feel left out at a funeral – the cards are more likely to go to your other parent than to you. This was something that Stephen found disconcerting, although his mother's funeral was well attended and so something of a comfort.

> People did talk to me, but kind of casually – I felt I was a bit of a sub-stitute for Dad; I felt they talked to me because they didn't really dare go up to him, or it wasn't going to pain me as much as him. And yes, it was a bit odd having all the sympathy cards addressed to him, and hardly ever to my brothers and sisters and myself. We felt a bit in the background, as though it wasn't really our affair.

Any details that can be gleaned about your lost parent remind you that he was a person, not just a father – they present perhaps a more rounded figure than the one you knew. Part of grief, and part of growing up, is learning to accept that our parental figures were indi-vidual adults. In fact, as time goes on, a certain lack of knowledge about your dead father is one of the most enduring features of grief. It does help a great deal if you have old friends or family members prepared to talk about him and his life.

Just after the funeral can be a difficult time, especially if your routine has revolved around a dying father for a while. Suddenly there is no one to visit any more, no more nightwear to bring home from the hospital to be washed, no more wondering if such-and-such a drink or food would tempt a fading appetite; you can pass a flower stall without wondering which type would be best to buy today. If your father has been ill even for a short time, you will probably have built up some kind of tenuous routine around this – it is easy to cling to its tiny details. They are after all a last link with your father.

Immediate mourning

Immediate mourning here means roughly the first two years following a bereavement – later chapters in this book take a look at longer-term reactions. It should be said, though, that while some people find that two years is a realistic appraisal of the time it takes to live through the strongest of their grief, it can take longer for others. Chapter 6 looks at factors which delay or complicate mourning.

Perhaps our first, most bewildering reaction is the difficulty we have in accepting the death of someone close to us. It means that, for a few days or sometimes longer, we just cannot take in the fact of death – we keep expecting to see the person pop his head round the door or walk up the garden path. The parent's death can be linked either to fears of separation we may have had as children or to experiences of actual separation, such as being left at a childminder's or at school. A child has a deep instinct to cling close to the source of survival; part of bereavement on losing a parent is to learn that that source is no longer appropriate as a survival mechanism for us. As adults, we can fend for ourselves, no matter what lingers in the subconscious from childhood.

The feeling that the dead person is still around can be very strong. People have reported 'hearing' the voice of the dead person, perhaps calling for a drink in the middle of the night; or may go up to his bedroom strongly expecting to find him in the bed, almost seeing him in the contours of the bedding. Linked to this is what is actually quite a common phenomenon – catching glimpses of the dead person.

A few days after her father's death, Hazel walked into the sitting room to see him smoking his pipe in his armchair, as usual. The vision vanished after a few seconds.

This is a typical report – the sight of the dead person is seen for an instant only. Others may report feeling someone touch them or brush by them, or smelling – Hazel could actually smell the tobacco Bob was smoking. It may be no more than a very strong feeling that the person has not yet quite departed. Incidentally, in other cultures, the strong sense of the dead person's presence is explained by the simple fact that the spirit does linger for a few days. Our own psychological jargon calls it denial.

Where have they gone?

This is the eternal question: what becomes of the personality after death? It's a question which develops the bewilderment touched on in Chapter 3 as to what becomes of someone's smaller as well as bigger characteristics.

After her mother died, Moira would sometimes go into her room and open the wardrobe which still contained all her clothes. She was struck by the faint perfume which lingered on, when the physical body of her mother had been cremated weeks before, and just could not reconcile the two facts with each other.

There is also the primitive infantile need to cry out to the dead parent, to alert him or her, just as an infant cries out to alert a sleeping parent (dead to the world, as it were). Some people have experienced crying in their sleep, or waking to find themselves with their father's name on their lips, sometimes years after the death.

While on the subject of sleep, dreams of the dead person should also be mentioned. One dream which has been reported a few times is of the dead mother or father trying to make a phone call to their child, but often having difficulty in speaking when the receiver is picked up, the voice becoming a squeak or a whisper. Others have reported even more disturbing dreams or nightmares.

> Michael would dream of his father and wake up in terror at the force of Tom's anger and rage which in the dream seemed to be fully directed on to him. He would also dream of meeting Tom's corpse – the funeral, with Tom's coffin being lowered deep into the ground, had horrified him. Janie dreamed of a malicious mother, who would mock her bitterly until she awoke in tears. Moira dreamed repeatedly of losing a tiny baby somewhere and of finding it eventually dead, shrivelled up, or turned to a small, broken wooden doll. (At this time, Moira was thinking of starting a family but felt unable to go ahead because her mother's death a year previously was still hanging over her.)

All these dreams persisted for up to five years after the event, most strongly in the first couple of years, and then diminishing gradually.

Sadness

Along with all the other, often complicated reactions to your parent's death, the utter sorrow that follows such an event is to be expected. But, some people aren't prepared for feeling this poignant grief to such a degree, or for so long. It's the way sadness sweeps through almost physically to the exclusion of other emotions. There's sadness for the past, for childhood, for all the memories of the different family homes and holidays we shared. Our link with this past has now gone. Shared jokes, nuances of communication with someone we knew longer and better than anyone else (and who knew us) have also gone. We also feel sad for the parent who is left, feeling his or her sorrow as well as our own.

It can be a relief if you acknowledge this emotion in all its powerful simplicity, and part of doing so is crying.

> Michael would often find himself in tears for his father for up to a year

after his death. His crying might arise from his train of thought, or it might just sweep in on him unexpectedly. He still cried in the second year, but less frequently.

Crying comes easily to some people, not to others. What can be frightening about crying out sadness for a parent is the way your own personality can seem to crumple into that of a child again; the adult concept of time melts away, and the overpowering present submerges you. The one person who could comfort the grief away in this infantile state is not there to do so.

Sadness easily merges into self-pity: who's going to look after me now? Even if you've been independent for some years, you may not have realized how much you took for granted the fact that your parents were alive, there if you needed them. Even if you have only lost one parent, this centre is destroyed, although a new centre may well form in time to come – perhaps within your own family unit, perhaps in that of a sibling.

Anger

When dealing with anger, it is helpful to accept first that it is a normal part of bereavement and second that there is a possibility that it may be clouding your judgement. The blaming of the medical profession, which began in your parent's illness, may continue; for a while, you may hate the doctors and nurses who cared for your parent. Anger can also be strong at people who still have their parents and live on in happy ignorance of the blow that has hit you. Above all, this can raise the hackles of envy.

> Anita felt her contemporaries just didn't understand and that this lack of understanding made them appear insensitive. All around her, it seemed, friends were visiting their parents at weekends, and having a two-day refuge from the all-too-real world; mothers were helping daughters plan their weddings or inspect flats in which to live. Although one part of her knew these friends were only going about their normal lives, the other part was furious at their self-satisfaction and lack of awareness.

Anita did have a self-confessed, innate tendency to envy in any case, and bereavement does accentuate such characteristics. In fact, we may be shaken at how destructive and deep our anger can be – how ragged and messy.

> Moira cut and tore up all the hand-made silk handkerchiefs she had inherited from her mother in a fit of rage one day. For some years, this

episode remained one of the most painful memories of early bereavement. Moira continued to be plagued by outbursts of rage for some years which were the more intense perhaps because she and her mother had experienced such a calm, tranquil end to Susan's life. Any feelings of anger towards her mother at dying had had to be repressed until after her actual death.

It is hard to accept how furiously spiteful it is possible to feel at the person who seemed to 'choose' to leave us: to wilfully and wantonly go off on some personal and private quest of their own volition. Most people do find it easier to express anger at something or someone else, whether it's hospital management or the Church of England. Anger at the dead person does exist after any bereavement but is a natural part of a parent's death.

Guilt

To some extent, it is possible to experience 'survivor guilt' after any death even if it wasn't part of some disaster. There may also be the 'if only' feelings to deal with, usually centring round what we perceive as sins of omission: if only we had called the ambulance an hour earlier; if only we had persuaded Mother to give up her job last year; if only we had been able to push our parents into moving to a better climate, as they'd vaguely planned . . . Surely there must have been something we could have done? Survivor guilt, however, argues that we still consider ourselves as responsible and powerful in the face of death, even though all the evidence is to the contrary. When we're used to making life better by our own efforts, it can be hard to let go and admit that there was nothing we could do.

This kind of guilt can be less potent after a parent's death because, as stated earlier, it is in the natural order of things for parents to die before children. Paradoxically, we may also feel it the more just because a parent has 'gone ahead' and taken advantage of his weakness. Our guilt that our father has gone may be accentuated by a certain relief that it *was* his generation's turn, and not ours.

Linked to this is a certain uneasy feeling reported by some that your own need to live somehow contributed to your parent's death – what could be called 'the Pelican Complex', after the young of the pelican who were reputed to drink their mother's blood! Moira was particularly conscious of this.

Until Mum got ill, I was quite eager to get married and have a baby – we had a wedding date all lined up which she didn't live to see. I feel a bit superstitious about my plans – as if by planning my life, I was being too selfish for her. My plans, my wanting to push forward, took too much of her energy. At a time when she was finishing with life, I was getting on out there. I had a need to live, she had a need to die – neither of us could change but the contrast made me feel very guilty.

The fact that the death of a parent removes the buffering generation between ourselves and death can also mean that guilt blends into fear. 'It might be me next' is closely interlinked to 'It could have been me then.'

We also have to come to terms with guilt because we haven't been good enough children. The child's self-centredness can be profound – that feeling that you're somehow responsible for everything, and that if your father is in a bad mood, it's directly due to you. After your father's death, memories take on a special sting – all the times you stayed out late or didn't do well at school or mixed with unsuitable company; all the quarrels, the resentments, the fault-finding. Try and keep this in proportion – some rebellion is a healthy part of growing up and if there have been genuine personality problems, guilt can both cloud the issue and keep you paralysed. Powerful emotion though guilt is, it doesn't necessarily spur you into action when it comes to moving on or to sorting out personal problems. As with most other stalemates in grief, talking to someone you trust can help.

We have had a profound influence on our parents, but it's important to remember that this influence is limited and also that our parents are probably more tolerant of us and our shortcomings than any other people. But, in addition to feeling guilty over the life we shared as parents and children, the time around the death can be very sensitive as far as guilt is concerned. Little things can be a bother for years.

Anita always regretted that, when the ambulance arrived to take her mother to hospital for the last time, she didn't pop back for the book her mother was reading at the time because she didn't like to ask the driver to wait. Anita's guilt was mixed with deep sadness – at this stage neither she nor her mother knew that this trip would be the last one.

Anxiety

Anxiety takes many forms, some physical (see below). What has happened to the person, originally responsible for *your* safety, can make you feel unsafe at a profound level. This can be one reason for insomnia: the feeling that it isn't safe to go to sleep, that it might be possible for you too to drift off into death as soon as unconsciousness comes. Of course, you may not experience anything as definite as this: merely a feeling of being somehow too stretched to sleep. These night-watches, in which you don't feel like reading, can be truly miserable. However, some form of exercise during the latter part of the day can help – an early evening swim, for example, or you could also make yourself get up and have a warm drink or bath – not so much traditional remedies for sleeplessness as just a way of passing the time. If you can't sleep, at least rest.

Exercise, and taking care generally of yourself, can also help combat the feeling about your physical body which can develop after a death. This is the feeling that your body simply isn't to be trusted, a deep physical dread of it falling apart – the more so because we came out of our parent's bodies: the ones which *have* ceased to function. If we lose weight after the death, it can be easy to fear we're becoming skeletal, and hard to share such a thought for fear of being labelled 'neurotic'. Although such thoughts are natural, it is important not to give in to them. Exercise may help (a few lengths in the local pool, for example): not only can it convince you of your physical soundness, it can also help you avoid some of the manifestations of physical grief.

Physical grief

Although grief is not an illness but a normal life event, it is possible to experience it physically. Grief absorbs large amounts of energy, leaving you run down and more open to illness – in particular, symptoms which mimic the disease of which our parent died.

> After Hazel's father died of bowel cancer, Hazel began experiencing stomach problems – loss of appetite, constipation and diarrhoea. Luckily she had an understanding doctor who was able to relate her increased visits to her father's death and once Hazel herself understood this she was able to accept and improve her poor health.

Hazel also had to make an effort to eat properly, something she found difficult after watching her father's appetite diminish over the weeks. Panic attacks were another symptom of grief.

> Once her major health problems had been sorted out, Hazel never thought to connect her grief with other distressing symptoms: mainly that she couldn't breathe properly and felt she had a lump in her throat. She also felt giddy enough sometimes for her head to spin. Once again it took hospital tests to make her understand that these were

manifestations of grief, in this case delayed for a few months after her father's death.

Do get such symptoms checked out with your doctor if you are worried – apart from anything else they *may* need minor medical help.

Going off course?

Your progress through life is interrupted profoundly by a parent's death. The first couple of years of mourning can sometimes take the form of what traditional mystics call 'the dark night of the soul'. It can be a period of emptiness, of dryness or of bleakness, in which all life and all hope seems to be suspended. Only much later can any value be seen in this period, when apparent spiritual torpor is often the covering for new growth. During this time, people may feel they go off course for a while – for example, taking an apparently unsuitable job.

Colin, a rather flamboyant actor, turned his back on his profession after his father's death and took a teaching job in a dull girls' school which was, his friends felt, quite out of character. Later, this 'year out' was something of a mystery to Colin. He could only explain it in terms of his need for isolation after his father's death. Because of the raw sensitivity of those first two years, Colin felt he couldn't bear the pretence implicit in his profession – he just wanted to put his head down and hide as much as possible from the world.

Delayed grief

Grief which is not fully lived through at the time can stop you from moving on. With our cultural dread of expressing emotion, we aren't always best prepared for the force of our grief, for its overwhelming nature. It seems to demand too much for too long; the changes it initiates are too sweeping. Grief demands that we move on from the life and selves we have hitherto known. This can be enough to frighten some people into not facing grief. There can be an urge to stay put as much as possible, even though new lives, new selves, do await those who can face their pain.

Other factors can delay grieving apart from a person's emotional make-up, notably important life events, such as getting married and having children (see Pregnancy). If grief for a parent hasn't been fully lived through at the time, it may strike later at another bereavement – sometimes as much as 20 or 30 years later, when a spouse dies.

Pregnancy

According to some researchers, pregnancy forms a special time when normal mourning reactions are unable to take place. The woman is said to be so preoccupied with the new life within that she cannot focus on the death of a parent enough to grieve. What is happening in her own body is too extreme in its opposition to death. Problems then start after the birth, often with a bleak post-natal depression compounded by not having your parent around to support you as much as you had expected. Certainly, there is an especial poignancy in not being able to share your new life with the person who gave you life.

> Michelle learned that she was pregnant in the morning, and in the evening hurried round to the hospital to tell her mother, only to find that she had died.

It is as well to bear in mind, however, that pregnancy and birth are times of unpredictable emotions – the 'right' feelings may not surface after a birth. In addition, there are what could be called natural mourning processes during pregnancy anyway – the gradual farewell to the self you were, the leaving behind of a familiar life for the unknown. This process intensifies after birth as you adjust to your new role.

However, if you find yourself suffering from post-natal depression – something which may well be contributed to by unassimilated grief – remember that it is treatable. Ask for help from your doctor or contact a special support group (see Useful addresses).

Taking a break from grieving

Grieving is hard work and, as with any work, you need time off. You will probably find this occurs naturally – you 'forget' for a day or so, and then it all comes flooding back. But, try and cultivate the ability to put grief aside from time to time if you can. It is not being disloyal to your parent – those memories will always be with you. It is being disciplined enough to go for a walk instead of sitting around, to seek company when you know you are really strong enough to take it now, to re-paint the kitchen. It is humanly impossible to feel pure emotions for long periods of time.

Some people have also found that, once the initial shock is over, a holiday can help. Again, it isn't possible to predict a good time to go on holiday – like everything else, it depends on your personal state. One aspect of going away can be that it enables you to devote time to people whom you've been neglecting because of your father's illness and death; however, a holiday can make grief both more and less painful.

Michael took his wife and children away a couple of months after Tom died so they could all spend more time together. He found this restorative – also the beautiful scenery around them. However, the pureness of nature also seemed to act as a pure channel for his grief, and he felt heartwrung in a way he hadn't when surrounded by the daily distractions of everyday life. The whole family did however enjoy this time together – a break in which they could start to settle down and start thinking about their own lives again, for the present and the future.

6

Patterns of loss

There are four main factors which affect the way in which you react to your loss: how a person died; the quality of your relationship with the person; the support you have during grief; and your experience of loss in the past. There is also your life situation to consider – if your life is still evolving, or is involved with other significant events, mourning can be affected. Chapter 5 traced the basic outline of grief; this one looks at influences on grief, and at the nature of loss.

There can be a fine line between 'normal' and 'complicated' grief. Grief feels so abnormal anyway, crashing its way into our life, destroying our assumptions and prospects. People's lives are not often simple enough to make the death of a mother or father the only event in them. People move house, have babies, get involved in car accidents, suffer problems at work, cope with debt, and so on, no matter what. But, a person's situation in life can complicate mourning: other deaths; major life events; jags in your own personality; unresolved complications in your relationship with your dead mother or father, can all make grief longer or more complicated. If this all sounds sombre, the positive side is that these added difficulties often spur a person into taking the initiative, pushing us over the edge of an old life and into a new one. If asked in advance, we would probably say we just wouldn't be able to bear it; but people do not only bear but triumph under a combination of events which they would previously have deemed catastrophic.

Other losses soon after your parent's death

Having to go through two bereavements around much the same time can prolong mourning. You may well feel numb to one, unable to take it in, or it may jolt you into mourning the earlier death in a way you may not yet have been able to.

Anita, who lost her mother, also lost her grandmother some months later. As her grandmother and she had been very close, Anita felt that this really was goodbye to her childhood and to any mothering she might expect.

It is worth noting that the other deaths don't have to be of people: the death of a pet can be a real tragedy in some people's lives – in a few cases, an escape from the other death which has occurred.

This is an example of the way in which grief can be deflected: we focus on the smaller loss because the other one is just too big for us to deal with yet. The same mechanism can operate with other losses which also occur soon after our bereavement; we may feel inordinately sad, for example, at failing an exam, losing a job or breaking a friendship.

> Jackie's friends were surprised at the way she reacted to a break-up with a new boyfriend. The relationship had barely been established, yet she seemed disproportionately upset about it until one friend, more discerning and braver than the rest, told her she was probably mourning more for her father's recent death than for her boyfriend.

The departure of certain hopes can call for mourning, too. The death of a parent usually leaves us in search of a new identity: but what happens if the role we hoped to fill is in the end barred to us?

> Ruth, whose mother died so unexpectedly as a lorry unloaded a skip, had to face another loss at the same time: she was told definitively that she would not be able to have a baby, after years of waiting and fertility tests. Her job of mourning was doubled: not only did she have to grieve for her mother, but for the motherhood she herself would never have, and for the children she would never bear.

Ruth's story is an example of the way the death of a parent can be the death of the past indeed, the ending of a chapter. Along with other circumstances, a parent's death can effectively cut a life in two, resulting in a completely new mode.

> As a health visitor, Ruth found that her infertility, combined with the terrific shock of her mother's death, had other effects on her; she no longer wanted to work with other people's children. She also wanted to move, because she and her husband had bought a large house with a garden some years previously on the assumption that they would soon be having a family. Although Ruth could not accept her situation entirely, she was robust enough to rise above it to a very large extent. She and her husband did move to a smaller place, and Ruth changed career direction, gaining a high-powered executive post for a large charity.

It's important to bear in mind that such changes don't happen all at once – you may still need to go through the exhausting process of grief before you have the energy to initiate such moves. Don't try and force the pace – in the scheme of things, a year or two is not that long in such major transitions.

Earlier loss

Your progress through bereavement can be affected by your experience of earlier loss. Because the death of a parent can so easily make us feel like children again, it is that much easier for it to trigger the feelings of fear, anguish and helplessness we may have felt when faced with, say, the death of a grandmother or the news that Father had left home either because of divorce or death, and wasn't coming back. But, loss in childhood may not be anything this stark. It may have to do with losing a pet, moving house, going to school, enduring the temporary absence of one or both parents – definitions of loss are varied and individual. Whatever the loss, it tends to be felt more in childhood, partly because we don't as children have that much power over our lives. Even without the desolation caused by the death of a parent, loss can be a feeling of emptiness, even of romance or glory passing away, which we don't as yet have the life experience or resources to fill.

> Hazel was profoundly disillusioned at around the age of ten when her grandparents moved from their cottage in the country to a suburban villa. She had lost a huge, overgrown garden and adjoining field – a child's garden of paradise – and the freedom to wander round the surrounding countryside. She also lost a pair of grandparents who up until then had been a rather fairytale means of escape from Hazel's native Liverpool.

An important feature of loss in childhood can be how our parents helped us deal with it – indeed how they can be implicated with a loss or even be the cause of it. Such memories can be very revealing – it is worth emphasizing, the loss itself may not actually be a very great one.

> As a very young child, Anita remembered how her mother threw out a doll as being too ragged and filthy to carry round any longer. Anita could recall vividly the sense of misery with which she saw the despised doll disappearing into the rubbish bin.

This incident, trivial enough from an adult viewpoint, had significance for Anita because it was bound up with the general ongoing sense of frustration and battle she experienced in her relationship with her mother. It wasn't the event, but the way it was conducted. Of course, some mismatch is to be expected between the expectations of children and their parents – neither side can get it right all the time.

Nevertheless, Anita felt moved to analyse the doll incident after her mother's death.

> It created in me a feeling that my mother was someone who was in charge of loss, like a god – rather terrifying, and even more terrifying when, seeing her dying, you realized that it just wasn't true. You don't realize you have these lifelong assumptions of your parents and the way they behave, until they die.

An ongoing insensitivity or clumsiness about a child's feelings, a lack of awareness as to how they experience loss, can become implicit in the parent–child relationship, having inevitable repercussions when such parents die. This is particularly true if your father coped badly with loss himself.

> Michael remembered how Tom had bungled affairs when a favourite family dog was put down. First, he didn't tell them for two days but let them assume the dog had wandered away from home. Then, he got drunk and blurted the news out in tears until most of the family were also in tears around him. Memories of this bathetic incident returned to Michael at Tom's own deathbed, adding to his feeling that Tom was not really equipped to deal with his own death.

Loss of a parent in childhood

> Jonathan was told that his mother had gone away for a while, whereas she had been killed in a car crash when he was seven. Therefore his grief – which he felt he wasn't supposed to have – was strictly private, and something of this permeated his entire life. As an adult, he rarely spoke about his mother, saying that there was no need and that it hadn't affected his life. He was the stiff-lipped Englishman *par excellence*, dogmatically matter of fact, tending to say, 'Everything will be all right', even when there was evidence to suggest otherwise. It was only when his father died that Jonathan was forced to realize that he had double mourning to do – that his father's loss triggered off all the feelings of desolation and loneliness he had experienced at his mother's loss.

The loss of a parent in childhood is one of life's better-studied tragedies, and many researchers have pointed out how damaging the long-term effects can be, especially if it happened when the child was under ten. A greater tendency to low self-esteem, depression and nervous break-down have all been cited as persisting effects. Some believe, however, that too much emphasis on this is unfair to those who were bereaved in such a way; focusing on the adverse effects doesn't really take into account a person's possibility for recovery and growth. (For more information about losing a parent or other loved person in childhood, you might find another Sheldon title helpful, *Helping Children Cope with Grief*, by Rosemary Wells.)

The death of other family members

When other members of the family have died in childhood, your security may not be undermined in the same way as when a parent dies. Nevertheless, the death even of a distant relation means a change in the world as you knew it and in your emotional status. In a way, an earlier death can be helpful in preparing you for your parent's death – it doesn't help with the grief, but perhaps the shock isn't as great as it might otherwise have been.

> By the time her mother died, Moira had also lost two grandparents, an aunt and a schoolfriend. In realizing that death was a part of life, she felt she had acquired some valuable knowledge, even though this was no consolation when her mother died. But, after a while, she did find it comforting to think that so many people had 'gone ahead' of her – that death was not as it were an 'unpeopled country'.

This depends on the nature of your attitude to an afterlife but while the death of a parent removes the buffer between yourself and death, it can for some people be reassuring to think of a loved one having accomplished what yet lies ahead of you.

Loss of a sibling can be another factor which affects your attitude to your parent's death.

> Clare's childhood was overshadowed by the death of her brother, when she was ten. Clare's parents always upheld him as a bright, promising boy – a shining star against which she couldn't hope to compete. When her parents died within a few weeks of each other, all her former feelings of sorrow, guilt and rage were re-activated. She was also conscious of a certain relief – that her parents had gone to join her brother at last and that she was free to get on with her own life, instead of bearing the burden of their sorrow and thwarted expectations.

What if you were lied to about death as a child? Parents use different ways of explaining death to children at different ages – for example, a very young child might need to visualize death as a different country far away. But, if you weren't told the truth about death at an age when you could have accepted a more mature explanation, this can add to the unease and mystery of the event when your mother or father comes to die.

Guy lost an aunt when he was about 12. His parents did inform him, but told him it was a heart attack. It wasn't until many years later that Guy discovered that it had in fact been suicide. When the 'little lies' technique was used later, as Edward was dying, this earlier incident added to Guy's anger and grief.

Not giving the full truth about death can be part of a more general ambience in which parents aren't really frank with their children – certainly true of Guy's family situation, which was discussed in Chapter 1.

Divorce or separation

A relatively new – and increasing – phenomenon today is the fact that a parent's death can trigger the pain of a specific loss earlier in life. This is the loss caused by separation or divorce in a family, when one of the parents often does pass out of the child's day-to-day life. He or she may not actually be dead, but it's a kind of death to the child, who sees far less of one parent on a day-to-day basis. Certainly the only family life the child knew has passed away.

Julia's mother and father had been divorced since she was 11. When Julia's father Martin became ill at the age of 77, her mother had either a slight stroke or some form of nervous breakdown. The doctor's uncertainty about the diagnosis didn't help at this traumatic time, in which Julia's mother retreated into the past and became very difficult to manage. When her father eventually died a few years later, Julia was hit by the need to mourn not only his passing away, but the earlier loss occasioned by divorce. The pervading sense of silence and desolation in the house, a sense of being horribly cut off from the outside world, of stasis without the possibility of moving on, were just as powerful on her father's death as when he had left all those years earlier.

Such an experience can pose a frightening threat to your identity. To have events return you thus to the unhappy past can leave you with the feeling that all the years in between, with their many achievements, have been invalidated; maybe that you've hardly moved on at all from the pain and confusion of earlier loss.

Perhaps the main need is to allow yourself to feel these feelings – all of them. Anger and bewilderment do not make for comfortable living, but the prospect of them is often more frightening than the actual experience of them. If you let them run their course, you will discover that they do have limits, but you may well need support to do this – another person, probably a trained counsellor, can act as a valuable safety net.

Earlier loss can also leave your relationship with your other parent soured – it is hard to avoid the goody–baddy syndrome in divorce. Julia, for example, was left feeling bitterly angry with her mother for what she saw as always escaping – first through divorce, then through illness, so that Julia and her sister were, as Julia felt, left with the whole burden of coping on their own.

Parents and prison

Another, rarer event which can evoke the same response is when a parent goes to prison. As with a violent or abusive parent, there may be the need to mourn what you never had – a strong, supportive parent and a stable family life.

Mary never got over her father going to prison when she was nine – her security was shattered for life. She might have got over an isolated incident, but he repeated his offence (pilfering) and was jailed a few times until Mary was around 12, when he managed to stop with the help of a good prison psychiatrist. In later life Mary was able to understand her father's actions as attention-seeking behaviour caused by unhappiness – but the emotional scars, though overcome to quite a large extent, could not entirely be done away with. Later, her father's death evoked the same reactions as she'd had when he had gone to prison. When the father departed, the home order was upset and the house felt less safe. There was also the social stigma, the feeling that she was cut off from other 'normal' people.

Losing your mother or father early in life

'Early in life' depends to a large extent not on age but on the stage you have reached in it. A 21-year-old who's happily settled in a marriage with the job of her choice or her own baby may feel more advanced in life than a 29-year-old who hasn't yet met the right man or isn't sure of her career. It very much depends on what you have yet to achieve, and how dependent you have been emotionally or materially on your parent.

Guy at 21 very much felt that he couldn't have lost his father at a worse time – just when he was about to leave university to start out in life, a time when he felt he needed his father to talk about all the decisions that faced him. Also, his father had promised him some letters of introduction to friends abroad, and there had been an idea that Guy might have tried to find a job among some of them. So, Guy felt his father's death had narrowed his horizons in more ways than one.

Guy took a job locally in order to be near his mother for a while. However, another complication was that he didn't get on with his boss, whose abrasive attitude contributed to the sombre mood of the next year. In Guy's case, the difficulties so many graduates experience in their first job were a considerable factor in his unhappiness over his father. He also felt that he was indulging in selfishness and in immature dependency. From this point of view, however, all grief is selfish and it is natural to want a parent's support when launching out into life.

If you do lose your parent early in your life, the chances are that it's relatively early in their lives, before the expected 60-plus age bracket. This involves what could be called unselfish grief – mourning for the opportunities you feel your parent has lost, for the years he never now will live. This isn't just retirement plans.

Guy's father Edward, who had married young, was in fact just 47. His death interrupted not only his career as a business lecturer, but all sorts of other plans. Now that Guy and the other children were grown up, Edward and his wife had had plans to travel, possibly to buy a second home abroad. Guy was, naturally, bitterly sorry to see the truncation of such plans.

Grief for your parent's life

Mourning for what should have been the dead parent's future also leads to mourning of his past – an area where it might be wise to beware of too strong an attempt at empathy. Apart from anything else, we simply don't know all the facts, and it may well be that our grief gives us a distorted picture of our parents' lives, especially at first.

Guy now felt that his father had spent his whole life with his neck in the halter, without ever quite reaching the rewards of his labours or achieving his full potential. In the same way, Michael mourned the personality difficulties which had prevented his father Tom from living as full a life as he might have done.

In this mood, it is easy to feel that your parent's life has been futile, narrow, pathetic, nothing but a race for money, a race against the clock. Time brings a fuller picture. Guy, for example, was able later to see his father's life as busy, valuable and contented, if rather private. Michael also saw that Tom, with his ferocious sense of humour, had in fact managed to get quite a lot of fun out of his 72 years, despite his eternal dissatisfaction.

Any death leads you to question what a life has been for, or about – how much more so if it is a mother or father who has died. Give yourself time for a more positive picture to emerge, to counteract the rather bleak 'Was that all?' feeling of earlier mourning. In the long term, perhaps the 'mandate against judging' is more useful than being too contemplative about a life which was not yours, of whose details you will never be fully informed.

Seeking substitute parents

Looking for someone to replace your parent is a strong if unconscious urge which is more likely to strike if you have been bereaved early in life. It may be that you become closer to an aunt or uncle, or to grandparents if they are still alive, although it is often easier to find someone outside the family.

> Anita had quite a struggle with dependency when she made friends with an older woman in her office. In the desperate loneliness following her mother's death, Anita could not help attaching herself to her friend, accompanying her round the shops at lunchtimes and talking to her perhaps too intimately about her fears and prospects – in fact, treating her as a rather younger person would treat her mother. In the end, Anita felt guilty at the way she was absorbing her kindly friend's energy and time, and this feeling was one of the main things which spurred her into getting another job. However, it took Anita many years and some counselling to get over her tendency to dependence.

This may seem to present rather a grim prospect – working again and again through the weaknesses left by a parent's death. But, such work is not a waste of time, even if it seems to be getting you nowhere.

> Anita eventually found herself in the happy position of being able to give as well as to take, with a responsible job and an established if sometimes tempestuous relationship. 'It had to be gone through,' was her comment on her years of grief and uncertainty following her mother's death. 'It wasn't even that I'm the stronger because of it – I'm a different person, at least that's how I see myself!'

How much guilt and anger?

Guilt has already been mentioned as a normal component of mourning. It's that gnawing self-reproach which tells us there must have been something we could have done to prevent the death, or the focusing on all the little ways in which we may have failed to make our dying parent's last weeks and days more comfortable.

In time, a more balanced outlook usually emerges; we are able to forgive not only the event but *ourselves*, to see that we did do all we could, that our failures were more than outweighed by the loving intentions and anxious care we managed to give, and by the pain and helplessness we experienced at their suffering. However, if guilt was a strong part of the relationship with your parents before their death, there may be more work to be done before it's finally laid to rest. Guilt can also be a way of holding on to the event, or of trying to control it. Its range, if limited, is at least defined: you know where you are with guilt, and sometimes it takes some ruthlessness to throw away what has become a comforter and to move on. In the end, prolonged guilt is a refusal to accept that we were, after all, powerless over cancer, road accidents and death itself.

However, guilt can be fought; first by recognizing if it is inappropriate, and second by giving your mind a new 'set' – an exercise which may well have to be done quite deliberately. Perhaps you could write down a list of your guilty feelings (which probably look a lot less depressing like this) and, in a column alongside, what you actually did for your parent, as well as the tender feelings you had. The positive list should be longer than the negative. Be quite firm about pushing guilty habits of thought away, and replacing them with new, more positive ones.

What about anger? It is important to distinguish if possible between the anger of bereavement, and the life-long anger of some difficult relationships.

> Michael was an angry man, always champing at the bit in life. Perhaps because he was used to finding and expressing this emotion within himself, perhaps because Tom's death allowed him to express the sorrow and fear behind his anger, he actually coped quite well with his anger in bereavement, in the long term. Moira was normally a quiet, caring girl, but found herself driven to strange rages after Susan's death; these did gradually die down in intensity.

It is certainly not fair to blame yourself for feeling too much, or to be afraid of your rage. Until it happens, you may not know just how much anger the event has aroused in you, or how bitter and all-embracing it may be on some days. If you are worried by the depth or force of your feelings, try talking to someone else who has been through a bereavement – knowing that someone else goes through it too can make all the difference when it comes to forgiving yourself afterwards.

Estranged children

What if you have been estranged from your parents for some months or years before their deaths? This may be not just because of a quarrel but because you've been living abroad, or simply because life has taken you different ways. How you react to the death depends on the reason why you haven't been seeing them. It is possible to lose touch with parents just as we do with other people – because our interests aren't the same, we don't have that much to say to each other, the relationship seems played out, and so on. If the separation was one of avoidance, if there were relationship problems we were evading, then grief is likely to include a larger share of guilt and uncertainty as to identity.

Melanie had made a life for herself in Spain as an English teacher. Married to a local man, she'd just had her first baby and was expecting her mother to come out for a long visit when the news came that Sheila had just died. Sorting out their complicated relationship was something Melanie had always hoped to do and she had been even more firmly set on it now that she was a mother herself. Melanie hadn't realized how much her attitude to her mother had been a central point in her life, a fixed point to react against, as it were. 'I would always say, at least I'm not like Mum, I haven't stayed in rotten old England. Suddenly, that prop was gone.'

Such a job now has to be done alone, with all the attendant regrets at the wasted opportunities of the past, and all the confusion. The relationship that never was, or that could have been, needs to be mourned. It's a relationship that was never terminated, so you miss out on that need to say goodbye which is so important. How you handle this depends on individual circumstances.

Melanie, for example, made a 'pilgrimage' to England with her baby to see her mother's grave and meet relatives whom she hadn't seen for years, a process which helped her shed some of her grief because she felt she was facing the issue squarely for the first time. 'I was able to accept a lot more that Mum and I never did get on, and probably never would have, no matter what. She wanted me to be someone different –

I wanted her to be someone different. I hope now we can leave each other in peace!'

Sometimes, especially if it was the parent rather than the child who was estranged, it may just be a question of acceptance – an attitude which may come slowly and painfully.

Because of the family row, Michael's father Tom had seen very little of Michael's wife Joan and their children. Part of Michael's grief was coming to terms with the way the feud had been allowed to overshadow his family life in this way.

How death can spur 'bad behaviour'

A parent's death can sometimes trigger latent problems, or make existing ones worse, especially if it does happen earlier rather than later in life and you were perhaps still reliant on your mother always to bale you out of your troubles. Although this means a painful period for the sufferer, it can also have the good effect of forcing a crisis. This type of reaction can push a person into a complete reappraisal of his whole life.

Nicholas, already a heavy drinker, let his father's death spur him into an alarming dependence on alcohol. He had previously relied on his father, Graham, to 'rescue' him from the results of his sprees. Graham would often pay his debts and, more importantly, talk him through the guilt and remorse that followed one of Nicholas's binges. Now that Graham was dead, Nicholas experienced many life problems, culminating two years later in the loss of his job and the departure of his wife. Nicholas was forced to overcome his problem on his own, which he did, initially relying on group and individual therapy, but eventually moving away from both. In fact, in later years, he sometimes wondered if he would have managed his painful crawl to true independence if his father had still been alive.

Nicholas is in fact an example of delayed grieving – he found giving up drink was the hardest thing he had ever had to do in his life, harder even than losing his father, because, without alcohol, he had to face the emptiness and hurt fully for the first time. His story also underlines the dangers of turning to comforters such as alcohol and cigarettes after a parent's death – they may muffle for a while, but can't remove the need to grieve for ever.

In this kind of case, there may well be regrets later about 'unfinished business'. What can be done? Perhaps for some time there may be little that can be done. The most mature course is simply to live with this knowledge. If the personality problem has been recognized, if attempts have been made at change, later opportunities may offer to 'make good'.

> More mature and stable some seven years after his father's death, Nicholas was able to help his new wife through the death of her own mother. He was present at the death (he had avoided his own father's deathbed) and felt in this way he was making up for all the neglected responsibilities which had been too much for him with his own father.

If death is a relief

Death often is an immediate relief. When an illness has dragged on and on, you welcome the end. But, that first thankfulness that it's over at last doesn't make it any easier to have lost the person. You can be glad for him, but not for you.

But, what if you are glad to be finally rid of a parent? What if your own feelings towards your parents have been largely mixed with confusion and hatred, or if death rids the family of a bad-tempered bully or an emotional vampire? This isn't to say that you don't love a parent who is less than perfect, or who plays all sorts of unconscious tricks on you.

> Anita was always uncomfortable because her mother, while urging her to be sociable, didn't like her inviting her friends round to the house; Michael's father was by outside standards completely unreasonable in terms of what he demanded from the family, and what he gave back. Yet, both were wholeheartedly loved within their family circle.

Nor does this mean the normal feelings of ambivalence, that compound of exasperation and love which is peculiar to the family, or those remorseful rememberings of how you could have done better.

This section refers to a parent who has obviously been a problem, who has terrorized the family for years with emotional unreliability or physical violence. In those sad cases where there has been abuse, verbal or physical, the death of a mother or father can make their adult children feel safer than ever before. But, grief is not the less because of a certain relief that your parent is gone. As has been stated before, recovery from bereavement does depend on the quality of the relationship you had, and the complications of a poor relationship can make for much anguished heart-searching after the death. You also have to mourn for the relationship you never had, for the father or mother you would have loved to have loved.

Kathy's father had regularly beaten her as a child, and she grew up with the one ambition of getting away. When she was an independent, successful working woman, she kept her address and phone number secret from him, yet she dreaded his possible death because she knew it would be the end of any possibility of a reasonable relationship. When he did die, of liver failure, her overwhelming relief was only the beginning of years of working through this painful and complicated relationship. Like Nicholas, Kathy needed a lot of support in this process.

Prolonged grief

It's hard to put a timescale on prolonged grief. But prolonged grief may be in question if after two years the darkness doesn't lift. Or if that darkness doesn't lift at all, if you start to feel overburdened with the care of your other parent or simply unable to start your life again. In cases of prolonged depression, you should consider professional help; if your doctor fobs you off or tries to prescribe you anti-depressants (less likely now than in years gone by) consult a bereavement-support organization (see Useful addresses).

Prolonged grief is different from working through the long-term effects and implications of a parent's death, especially if it has happened earlier in life. Moira, for example, estimated that it took her seven years fully to come to terms with her mother's death; Guy, some ten years later, said he had never really got over his father's death. But, in the interim, both were able to pursue careers, to marry and have children – in a word, to go on living fully while sorting out the aftermath of their grief.

7

Inheritance: new possessions, new ideas?

Inheritance has a very wide meaning when a parent's death comes to be considered. Material and spiritual inheritance are closely intertwined – can it ever be just material? The clock inherited from your father, and perhaps from his father before him, has far more value than one bought in the shops. Since inherited objects are so emotionally loaded, it can be difficult to be objective about them (one reason why family rows over property can look so out of proportion to outsiders). The inheritance of possessions or money may bring strong feelings of ambivalence. It may feel wrong that you now own what was so recently the property of another person, and there may be a feeling of intrusion, especially if you have to go through things soon after the death when the presence of your dead parent still seems strong. There may be feelings of fear and sadness at the way death has scattered the structure of a lifetime – all the records, books, and pictures which were so carefully collected over the years, which made a home, have now lost their central value.

Deciding what to keep is a vital part of coming to terms with your parent's death and of forging your own new identity. It's important to remember that, poignant though the material remains of your parent's life may be, you are not obliged to hang on to any of them. What you keep can be an indication of how much of her lifestyle and way of being you want to carry on, and how much you want to strike out on your own.

There is also the inheritance of ideas to be considered – what you've inherited not just from your family, but in a wider sense from society. If, for example, you were brought up in some form of religion, you may well need to re-examine your thoughts and feelings on it. After a death is a very common time for people to either turn anew to some religion, in the search for meaning, or to turn away, feeling that it has failed them.

Also, fully accepting a parent's death involves accepting the reality of your own mortality. At some point, you may well benefit from sorting out your ideas about death in general. Reflections are bound to have been triggered by the event. The conclusions you come to are more developed than your previous ideas. Now can be a time for throwing out ideas that have been handed down to you – or for returning to them anew and remoulding your cultural inheritance to fit your own particular style.

Losing a part of yourself

Inevitably, losing a parent means losing a part of yourself: the flesh from which you came, if nothing else. But it's actually far more: you've lost someone who was greatly responsible for the moulding of your identity – you may even have depended on the identity which your father had of you, on his definition of you. You've also lost the person who had prime access to your childhood, who could pass on family memories; who knew, perhaps uniquely, how you'd changed and developed.

This can leave you unexpectedly blank about your earlier years. You've lost the person who could fill in all the details of those classic family episodes – what happened exactly the Christmas Gran burned herself cooking the turkey, the real reasons which lay behind the ancient row your parents had with your aunt and uncle.

You might also want to know some personal details which you were not previously told: at exactly what time you were born; how often you had tantrums as a child; or at what age you learned to read. Such questions often become more pertinent when you yourself go on to have children: there is a natural urge to check out their development with your own in your early years, or your children may ask questions about your own childhood.

If you've lost both parents, this knowledge may have been lost for ever. A surviving parent cannot always supply this information – maybe he doesn't remember, maybe you don't like to ask in case it raises memories of happier times. Fathers too are often vaguer about childhood details than mothers, who usually have spent more time with their children when small.

However, it's also important to remember that your identity isn't dependent on your parents, even if it started from them. In the end, it is up to you to pick and choose which parts of that identity you want to carry forwards into maturity. This may mean rejecting bits of family myth ('Anita's so impractical – can't boil an egg.' 'Guy would never make a good husband – his head's always in the clouds.'). You go on changing and developing in many ways after a parent dies, and indeed the death itself can easily spur you into outgrowing family labels. This is especially true if one or both of your parents died while you were still establishing your adult identity.

Something to keep?

Deciding what to keep and what not to keep is an important sorting out process after your parent's death. Bear in mind that, in the rawness of grief, you may want to push everything out of sight, to get rid of everything in the unconscious hope that you can sweep away some of your pain with it.

However, mementoes acquire more value with the years, and what causes you pain in the beginning will be a precious link in time to come. Try and make sure you have something to keep, however small. This can sometimes be difficult – it is common for people not to make wills, and even if they do, minor keepsakes can easily get left out. In this case, you may have to negotiate with other family members to obtain a memento. There's also the possibility that your other parent doesn't think of your need in this respect, and you may be afraid of asking for fear of being thought selfish, greedy or intrusive.

> Guy particularly wanted his father's watch, which had been inherited in turn from his father. However, his mother put all his father's possessions in his cupboard and shut the door. Three years later, his sister finally went through everything when their mother was moving house, but by that time Guy was living in another part of the country and no one thought to ask him if he wanted anything.

Going to the opposite extreme, the situation can arise where perhaps too much is handed on.

> Michael was given practically everything his father owned as his brothers were wealthy enough to need no more than a token each – while he was felt as needing it more, as youngest son and father of a growing family. He ended up with suits of clothes, a second CD player and TV, and other furniture. 'It was too much. Dad had such a strong presence. It was like having him in the house – I'd be almost seeing him there in his flat, old and ill, listening to his records or whatever.' Finally, Michael and his wife Joan went through everything, chose a few special items to keep, and gave the rest away.

As this story shows, there may be an underlying economic need which dictates which family member is given more. In times gone by, inheritance was a major way of coming by possessions, more so than we can perhaps realize in today's culture where we tend to buy what we need, saving up for a marriage bed rather than inheriting Gran's old one.

Deciding what to get rid of can be just as important in saying goodbye to your dead parent and in establishing your new identity.

> Margaret's elderly mother had always collected milk-bottle tops for the blind. When she died and Margaret went to clear out her house, the very first thing she did was to throw away every single top in the house!

This is where it can be helpful to have discussed with your father whether he wanted anything particular done with his effects. It is much easier to get on with it if you know for example that your father wanted all his clothes sent to a charity shop. Giving belongings away can also be made a valuable part of the mourning process, although it can pay to wait a while before you decide what to part with.

> Hazel gave away her father's old and valuable collection of annuals; at the same time, she gave away all her own childhood books. She felt that if she and Will ever had children, they would want to start anew, without the ghost of family memories. Later, when thinking more closely about a baby, she did rather regret this wholesale 'chucking out' – she felt she would have liked some of her books to keep for her own children, after all.

Although it can be a mistake to rush in and get rid of everything, hanging on to belongings can sometimes hold you back. Sorting through them does help you acknowledge at depth the reality of what has happened, to clear both mental and physical space for what is to come next. Although it's a painful task, it needs to be done before those untouched belongings acquire a kind of taboo from never being examined.

Benefiting by inheritance

How can you legitimately feel glad about gaining extra money from such a cause as the death of a parent? It is easy to feel ambivalent about bigger inheritances.

They may also raise many practical questions. For example, it is more common now to inherit property in a country where so many more people own their homes than formerly.

> When Jackie lost both her mother and her father, she was left a house and a substantial sum of money. Never a career girl, she now had no need to work, which actually added to the sense of isolation she felt after

her parents' death. An only child, she had never been close to the rest of her family, and at first she felt that the money had served to make her even more cut off from people, although she very largely overcame such feelings in due course with her established circle of friends and a happy marriage.

If you inherit property alone, you may either find yourself wealthier than you ever expected to be or you may end up burdened with the care of two mortgages for a while. A word of warning: unless you are very sure about it, think twice before giving up your own home and moving into your parents' house. There can be a strong desire to stay close to the family home in the first few weeks after the death, but in doing so permanently you may be giving up friends and connections which would be of more value to you in the long term than the increasingly tenuous links with the past.

Some people choose to convert an inheritance into a tangible and preservable asset, such as a house or a business. Helen, for example, chose to put her father's bequest towards a holiday home, so that it would be spent on something enduring, rather than being frittered away. Linda put the small sum her mother left her towards a publishing venture.

Sometimes inheritance can suggest other changes in lifestyle, even if you don't take them up. For example, you may inherit a business, or pieces of equipment which might give your work life a new turn.

Glen inherited his father's import business, and, after some indecision, decided not to sell it but to try and make a go of it. Colin inherited a computer which he used to get a presentation skills business off the ground – something he'd been pondering as a supplement to the uncertain life of acting but which might not have materialized without the computer.

But, it may not always be appropriate to hang on to inheritances. They may be a link with a past which really has little relevance to your day-to-day life now.

Clare inherited a small farm in Norfolk. At first she was determined to run this, but it soon became apparent to her that happy childhood memories of the farm were one thing, managing a business was another, especially in the wake of much bigger farms which were keen to buy her out. With her roots firmly in London, she decided that the healthier move was to sell.

Your inner home

One of the most important effects of losing a parent, in the long term, is that it leads you to find your own centre – the inner home without which you would be rootless. Achieving emotional independence from our parents is a process which takes place whether they die or not, but which is inevitably easier if they do. Stephen touched on this transition when speaking of his uncertainty as to where his home was now that both parents were dead.

> I eventually realized, after a few months, that it was up to me to make my own home now. I don't mean I rushed out and bought somewhere – just that I had to get used to thinking of myself as the source of security. There wasn't some long umbilical cord trailing back to Nottingham any more. Not that there had been really – only traces, but now even the traces were done away with.

Achieving your inner home marks the transition from being a receiver (the child whose duty it is to accept) to a giver (the adult whose duty it is to give). Passive becomes active: the person who has always attended family events may now become the one to initiate them; from going home every Christmas, you now move to being the one who's out there in the kitchen, cooking the turkey while the rest of the family clinks glasses in the next room. Being 'settled' in this way is a mark of the greater self-reliance that comes after a parent's death, though it may not come all at once, but gradually over a period of years.

It is in this sense that you become the 'culture-carrier' already mentioned in Chapter 5. It is now up to you to decide whether you even want to celebrate Christmas or not. There may be family traditions which you don't want to let slip, or you may want to continue or even expand on a parent's cultural interests – building on a parent's music or book collection, for example.

'First' death

For everyone there is a 'first' death – the first time that death becomes real to you. For many people, the first death is in fact their parent's, so that as well as facing the shock of losing someone so near, there is also the shock of confronting the unknown, the void. It's at this point you may realize the force of the truism that our society has segregated death, making it invisible in spite of its apparent daily appearance in the media. It is quite possible for people to reach their 40s and 50s without ever having seen a dead body. In reaction, you may for a while feel that this enormous black fact of death is the only reality, against which people rush about like 'oblivious ants'. Time will restore the balance to your outlook, but it does indeed take time to digest this gut realization of the reality of death.

Naturally, this isn't to say that you take any future deaths as a matter of course. Death is always death. But when it happens again it may not seem quite so blindingly impossible: you will have become familiarized with the effects of shock, grief and fear.

Attitudes towards death: inherited taboos

In theory, we know that our society ignores or avoids death. What isn't always easy to grasp is the emotional force with which its reality can hit you as a result. Imagine the shock, for example, if the same attitude applied to childbirth and you did not discover how babies were born until you found yourself in the labour ward. Though knowledge and preparation in both cases may not make going through the event any easier, at least some of the utter shock is taken away.

We cannot help inheriting these taboos to a greater or lesser extent. But, if it is difficult for our society to be open about death, how much more so within our immediate family! It is easier if the inevitable is accepted by all openly, with calmness and dignity. This may be possible for some families with strong religious beliefs and loving, mature relationships. For others, however, getting to that point may involve overthrowing so many family structures that it becomes impossible, as Guy found.

> I used to long for someone to say something – just one word – that would show they could admit to the truth. We all *knew* what the truth was – but no one would *say* it. I found that one of the hardest things of all, my mother trying to do the housework as normal and not seeming to have any time for death.

Guy felt this attitude denied them all something: one of the conclusions he came to was that death must have its place.

However, if communication is constricted about death, at least identifying your position can be useful. You are after all caught by a social taboo, a victim of an attitude that is none of your making. However, you can store the knowledge up for 'outside use' – later you may be able to find someone with whom to break the taboo. You may find that pain makes the barriers come down and that you are able to talk more easily within your family. Otherwise, don't force the issue – it may be easier to accept that it is just too painful to do anything about it within your own family. Frankness, however desirable it may seem, may just not be appropriate for now. Challenging the death taboo head-on with a grief-stricken parent may be more than you (or they) can bear.

Your own idea of death

You will probably need to look at other psychic inheritances at some point, especially if you have been brought up in a religious belief. It is true to say that your parent's death will be one of the biggest challenges to faith that you will ever meet; but it is also true to say that this is one of life's events that faith addresses.

Some people abandon religious faith on facing parental death but, before you reach this point, it might be worth talking to someone. If your local minister doesn't seem right, bear in mind that insight into these matters varies from person to person: someone else might be more suitable. For example, the hospital chaplain or priest is experienced in dealing with the kind of spiritual crisis you are going through, and would probably be able to recommend other people to contact according to your particular needs and religious background.

There is a fairly common phenomenon of people 'turning to religion' after a close death, and also wandering away again. There is an initial need to find meaning, to absorb the implications of the experience but, once this has been done, the mechanics of formal religion may still seem foreign, even if the seeker has caught some of the original spirit.

> Anita, a cradle Catholic, had not bothered about religion for many years. After her mother's death she did go back to the Church for about a year, but felt it did not have what she was looking for. She went instead for individual counselling, and later to a bereavement group, where she found the warmth that had been lacking for her in the Church. She did eventually make up her quarrel with the Church in the sense of taking some of the beliefs but leaving all the ritual. 'I don't go to church now, but I do have certain deep beliefs – I suppose most priests' hair would stand on end to hear me say that, but it's simple – I'm comfortable that way. I couldn't go back to church. It's too like going back into the past, I just can't do it.'

Whatever you believe, if you haven't had close experience of death before, the chances are that your faith, if you have one, and your own ideas of death, are inadequate for your present needs. For example, we tend to have a paternalistic view of God in our society ('God the Father' and sometimes 'Mary the Mother'). The implications of this need further exploration once our own mother or father dies. Both for now and for later, there is a need to make your own 'myth of death' – a private, personal view of death that isn't open to other people's scepticism or rationality. It isn't really a matter of thinking it through and deciding what you do and don't believe, nor need your myth be anything to do with literal fact. It's an overall attitude which is achieved quietly, with time, slow thought, reading and talking. In other words, it has to be lived through if the end-product is to prove inviolable. This kernel of experience can be one of the most valuable residues of a parent's death. While it can take many years to achieve, the earlier you can come to terms with death in your own way, the better.

To start this process, you may want to examine other people's ideas of death, past and present: the concept of heaven, for example; or the more recent phenomenon of near death experiences. Looking at other cultures may be a help. In Ancient Crete, for example, funerals were happy affairs during which the soul, freed from life, was pictured as being released into the blue sky. Without indulging in escapist spiritual fantasies, making your own private myth can help you assimilate the reality of death into your life.

8

You and your remaining parent

One particular effect of losing a parent is that there is another person left behind whose grief is usually regarded as being greater than yours. It can sometimes be difficult to handle 'selfish' grief when comforting your remaining parent – to act parentally and give love and support when you need parenting so much. Or, it can be a challenge to which you rise with new-found maturity. Also, some parents and children are drawn closer together by their grief and a strong feeling that outsiders don't really understand.

Apart from anything else, this can be a frightening responsibility – if, for example, you fear that your mother may commit suicide, or simply dwindle away and die, because she can't bear life without her partner. If you are truly afraid that this is a possibility, you can consult your doctor or social worker. You should remember that you can only do so much and that, in the end, you are not responsible for your other parent's life.

Even without such extreme fears, you still have to deal with a general change in your relationship. The balance can be a difficult one to achieve because, although you may well feel the need to be supportive, you can't overstep the parent–child boundaries. You can't suddenly start acting too parentally towards someone who has always parented you, even though you may need to take on more responsibility for her than ever before. It's a situation which needs tact because grief can leave people so stunned. Seeing your other parent so apparently helpless, it's all the more tempting to rush in with formulas for making it better – anything from a new hair-do to moving house. Sometimes, it needs to be remembered that another person's grief just can't be managed like this – grief needs to run its course and to try and distract your other parent before it's time just won't work. Also, it can be a refusal either to accept what has happened or to allow your mother to mourn as she needs. It's almost taking advantage of her sorrow in order to persuade her into courses of action which she might not otherwise have chosen.

After Tom died, Michael's brothers clubbed together and sent Michael's mother Gloria on holiday to the south of France. This well-meant bullying did little for her grief, and when she came back she went straight back to her house and refused to see anyone for a month.

Apart from anything else, your other parent is probably deeply tired, especially if she was involved in prolonged nursing. She needs time to recover from this exhaustion, which is just the beginning of the grieving process.

Alternatively, some surviving parents cling to their roles as fathers or mothers, and continue to look after you, being concerned about your feelings, instead of coming to terms with their own. This makes it even more difficult to give anything to your parent, and it can also be a source of regret later on to her – that you didn't all 'go through the death' with emotions shared more equally. Different families play at being strong in different ways. It can be very difficult for a parent (or a child) who has set up in this coping role to come down, to admit that he or she is just as grief-stricken as the rest of the family.

Your other parent may feel that he does now have a dual role – that his responsibility towards you has been doubled and that he needs to be both father and mother to you to make good your loss as far as possible. Having your other parent 'baby' you in this way – worrying about how you're taking it instead of how he is – offers the temptation to pretend that life hasn't changed as much as you know it has. So, you do sometimes need to be clearer-headed than your emotional needs dictate.

Moira's father, a gentle soul, had not liked her nursing her mother, especially when it had involved jobs such as helping with colostomy bags. Dick, it seemed, like to think of Moira as younger and less resilient than she really was – as a little girl, his little daughter. Although Moira would partly have loved to play the role of being looked after, she wasn't convinced. She felt Dick was glossing over his own grief in this way, even evading it, and that it deprived them of the chance to mourn together.

Finally, in some cases, the death of one parent doesn't make that much difference to the relationship with the surviving one. This can happen when parents and children lost real touch years back – or never really established it at all. However, part of grief in this kind of case can be mourning for what never existed – the deeper relationship with your surviving parent – especially as by now it may well not be possible to change the more superficial contact you have.

How much support?

I felt my mother was the only one who really understood. We didn't want to see anyone else – we needed to talk about my father. It was natural for me to stay at home with her until I got married – I wanted to give her that time, I felt I owed it to her. The support wasn't a one-way thing – we supported each other.

Following the death of one parent, there often follows a natural time in which, like Hazel, your relationship with your other parent becomes stronger, when outsiders are automatically excluded. Just being there for your mother is probably the best way of offering this kind of support, though it's important to remember that it can only be *offered*. Your bereaved mother may not be willing or able to take it, despite your endeavours. The loss of a parent or spouse, touching one to the core, is one of the most private griefs known, and tramping in emotionally is not always the answer. So, if your other parent doesn't want to talk about it, there is little that can be done. Silence may be your mother's best method of survival; all you can do is be ready to follow up any openings she may give. In the end, we all live alone with our own grief.

So, how much support can or should you give? What is support anyway? Must you be a substitute for the lost parent? How can you best help your other parent? Is it arrogant to even try and comfort her after such a loss?

Grief does absorb people to the core, perhaps making them appear self-centred, and it can be helpful to remember this for both of you in your daily dealings with your mother. It is important that you let her grieve in her own way and time.

On the most basic emotional level, it is difficult to accept that our parents, the gods of our childhood, can fail. Traces of childhood jealousy or insecurity can also make it difficult to accept that no one can be a substitute for the person who has gone. However, even if this were possible, it may well not be the healthiest option. People may spend their lives looking after a widowed parent, and there's more about the stresses this involves in Chapter 10.

From our point of view, it's also true that 'having to get on with it', being more responsible for another person, can go some way towards filling the vacuum of those first empty days and weeks. But, there has to be a balance between supporting your parent and expressing your own grief, especially if your experience is unlike Hazel's and you don't find yourself automatically drawn closer to your other parent. Research has repeatedly stressed this need to express grief – it isn't healthy to suppress it, to be too confident and coping. No matter how much you feel you ought to support your parent, you also need to acknowledge your own sorrow, to grieve with your parent, rather than being consciously and brightly 'supportive'.

Grieving together can be complicated by many factors: by your relationship; by the ups and downs of grief in your mother; by her (and your own) varying needs for privacy; and by any feelings you may have that her grief is more important than yours (or vice versa). With this in mind, perhaps the best 'support' that can be given is just 'being there' – not trying to be the perfect child, not trying to comfort grief away before it's time, and accepting the ebb and flow of grief in your other parent and in yourself.

Twice bereaved?

So, what if grief doesn't draw you and your mother closer together? Sometimes, it may just not be possible to reach your other parent, who shuts herself away with her sorrow. This is especially true if there has been a previous relationship of limited communication.

Guy felt that, in a way, death had deprived him of both parents. Not only did he have to deal with the loss of his father, but also with the 'loss' of his grief-stricken mother whom, after two years, he described as 'still very remote'. This led to feelings of resentment at his mother which Guy had no trouble in identifying as childish and irrational – even a feeling that his mother could have done more to prevent his father's death and had somehow acquiesced in it or was unconsciously responsible for it, though Guy did realize that this was his grief rather than an objective fact about his mother.

The course of relationships in grief is, naturally, going to cover the tracks laid down previously. One of the effects of this restrained kind of relationship, with your surviving parent, can be to make all the leftovers from childhood have their full impact – perhaps leaving you feeling that your emotions are unimportant or that your grief is nothing but childish self-pity in comparison with that of your other parent.

At times Guy even felt he had to suppress his own need to grieve in the face of one who so obviously had the right to be first mourner. If his mother didn't show her feelings, what right had he to come out with his? This feeling was compounded by one friend, who, when first told the news of his father's death, burst out, 'Oh, your poor, poor mother!' Guy felt that this was no doubt the right and proper reaction – but where did it leave him?

Allowing the grief to be devalued in this way, feeling that yours is 'inferior' to your remaining parent's (something which can have its roots in low self-esteem) is a humiliating experience which you really don't need. Who is going to measure grief? Unfortunately, this was an example of how a moment's thoughtlessness can grate on the sensitivity of the newly bereaved, sparking off yet more guilt. It took Guy many years before he could see his friend's comment for what it was – a thoughtless blurting out of what her feelings would be if she lost her own husband.

In addition, these feelings don't help your surviving parent either – they can even leave her more isolated than she would have been. You cannot place your other parent on a pedestal of grief; your grief *is* shared. But perhaps not all the way – you have to respect your other parent's privacy. It may be hurtful to be told 'You just don't understand', but it certainly doesn't help to be measuring who is suffering the greater pain. Apart from anything else, you and your mother (or father) are mourning different people: a spouse and a parent. Naturally, you cannot fully empathize with all the details of someone else's relationship. They have shared time: more time than your whole life; they have shared life experiences which you may yet have to go through, such as marriage, sickness, the birth of children. Your mother has lost the person with whom she lived on a day-to-day, physical basis – research has shown that one of the things missed most when a partner dies is touch. Older people especially, who live isolated lives, may go for months or even years without ever being touched after the death of their partner. Likewise, your other parent can't quite fully enter into what the loss of your father or mother means to you – the loss of security, the poignancy of all those childhood memories, the general farewell to your past.

Lifestyle changes

If death leaves your mother alone, the natural urge is to provide company for her, either by moving in with her yourself for a while or by having her come to live with you. However, you should give it time before making this a permanent decision. In general, people are advised not to make any major decisions until a year or two after a bereavement. Many a widow or widower has sold their old house soon after the death, only to feel regretful later on. When grief has lost its first edge, the memories associated with the old place become valuable rather than painful. Also, the old routine and familiarity can help someone live through their grief. So, it might be a good idea for your parent to pay you a visit of a few weeks first, before coming to any long-term decision.

However, there's also the possibility that your parent may be left in a house too large or expensive for him to manage alone: in which case an earlier move could be beneficial.

When Stephen's father died, he and his brothers and sisters sold the rambling old family home to buy their mother a small modern flat. The family was amazed at how much she enjoyed her new home and, once her initial grief was over, she seemed happier there than she had been for years.

Losing your 'favourite' parent

As well as being affected by a troubled relationship with the dead parent, mourning can also be complicated if you're left with the parent you feel less close to. This can be a chance to build a whole new relationship with your remaining parent. It isn't necessarily true that grief draws people closer together. It can be surprising how persistent old habits of communication – or non-communication – are.

Michael always felt his mother refused to talk on any but a superficial level with him. This didn't change after Tom's death, and Michael felt cheated of the long talks about Tom they could have had, of the memories she could have passed on.

In a wider sense, what happens if you lose the family 'communicator'? Often in a family, one parent (often but not always the woman) takes on the role of mediator between the different personalities in the house. He or she is the one who smooths everyone's path, who forms a bridge between parents and children, who explains motivations and diverts anger: the one who enables family life to run smoothly. When this is the parent who has died, the family status quo breaks up, either slowly or immediately. There follows a period during which the family may seem to drift apart, especially if the children are all adult and living their own lives. In time, one of the children may well find him- or herself taking over this role (or the different siblings will take on different parts of it) being the one to remember birthdays, to invite people for Christmas or to visit other family members.

Being left with your 'favourite' parent

Hazel, an only child, did have some ambivalence in her grief. She'd always been closer to her mother than her father so that, when Bob died, she also had to cope with a faint feeling of relief that 'at least it wasn't Mum'. In fact, her mother and she had had a habit of teasing Bob – ganging up on him, as he used to say. Now that he was dead, they were in the position of having to take seriously someone at whom they had spent much of life laughing.

When you've lost the parent you got on less well with, the traditional family structure needs a complete re-appraisal. Hazel, for instance, suddenly realized how a family tradition of mockery had given both her and her mother a kind of safety and had kept the relationship with her father on hold, stopping it from developing any further.

There may be a certain amount of guilt if you feel at all relieved that at least your 'favourite' parent was spared; this can be connected with jealousy if the surviving parent is grief-stricken by his loss. But this doesn't mean that your grief is any less genuine.

Expectations of your parent

It is easy, especially some time after the death, to have wrong expectations of your surviving parent – that he pull himself together, that he re-carpet the shabby hall, dispose of the dead parent's possessions or 'get on with' moving instead of just talking about it. If you don't live together, and you see him only on visits, all such things are likely to be more clear to you. It may be very much more difficult for your parent to 'get a move on' than you realize. Making a change – any change – is a deep admission that life goes on, an admission he may not yet be ready to make. It can take many months or years before your surviving parent is able to deal fully with his grief. He may need support, in varying degrees, *just as he is* during that time. To him, it may seem like a betrayal to move on or simply to make the final admission that death has taken his partner, that time will not bring her back, and that their shared past is to be 'desecrated' by a change or a move.

However, there may come a point when you sense that your parent would like to move on in some way, but can't quite do it alone and would perhaps welcome a gentle push. One way of tackling this can be with the help of siblings.

Moira and her sister put their heads together and decided that Dick wouldn't be averse to a good clear-out of all their mother's things. 'I would have been a bit chary of descending on him on my own and going through the house, but together it was no problem. We just sensed the time was ripe and events proved us right – he was definitely quite relieved when we took matters into our hands.'

Moira's comment raises a point worth noting – the signs your parent himself gives as to his readiness to move on. These may be just subtle hints, or plainer signs, like a move to sell the old house. But, this can need careful judging, as your mother may need to talk about her plans for some time before actually putting them into action. There is a difference between talking about selling the house and ringing an estate agent. You cannot do the entire job for her – only help out if she shows that she is ready to be helped.

Care of your surviving parent

Apart from emotional support, one of the most immediate ways in which you can help your remaining parent is on a practical level – making sure she eats, shops and generally looks after herself. A balance is needed if you're not to become intrusive and you have to judge how far to go. Do you want to move in for a while and look after your parent? Is it a case of weekly visits plus a trip to the supermarket? Will you make frequent phone calls to keep in touch?

If the dead person was always the one to take care of the practicalities, your help might be needed in a variety of areas, such as looking after the car, paying the mortgage or finding your way round the local shops. But, don't try and do too much – part of your surviving parent's readjustment must be learning to look after him or herself, in new areas if need be.

But for now, try and make sure your parent does eat properly, keeping stocked up with fresh fruit and sensible food – bring some yourself on visits and cook meals yourself, if it's appropriate. With fathers especially, it might be helpful to buy other basics which perhaps your mother always looked after – the mundane business of new socks, washing-up sponges, Hoover bags etc. A word of warning: be careful how much alcohol you bring into the house; it isn't a question of your parent becoming dependent on it, but the fact that even a couple of glasses can make him or her feel highly uncomfortable, causing him to feel all the sorrowful emotions more acutely and, perhaps, making him express them more freely than he really wants to.

Sharing the care

This partly depends on how much family you have and on how available they are. A sister with a new baby or a brother who lives in Australia aren't going to be able to contribute on the same scale as you if you're unattached and live locally. It is also possible for siblings to make their 'life situations' excuses for not helping more – they may feel too busy, even though it's probably an illusion in many cases. You may need to work out exactly how much help you can give, stating your position to other family members with a clear request for more involvement.

You also need to bear in mind your parent's own preferences, which can provide yet another occasion for sibling rivalry.

Colin, for example, felt disgruntled because his mother so obviously preferred to spend Christmas with his brother. Michael felt his mother could have visited his young children more often – she seemed to spend more time with his eldest brother's family.

All things being equal, if your family are nearby, fairly available and amicable, you should certainly make some attempt to share the care: do not take everything upon yourself when it comes to caring for your surviving parent. The pull towards caring for a bereaved parent is strong, but the pull towards living your own life also needs attention: if not right now, then hopefully in the future.

9

Help

As has already been stated, the help and support a person receives after a death can also affect the quality of bereavement. Once the initial isolation of grief has passed, you may need to talk about your lost parent and your experience of grief.

Perhaps you've already been able to do this within your immediate circle of family or friends. But there can also be a need for a more objective, deeper appraisal. This might be with people who know neither you nor your family, but who've been in the same position of losing a much-loved mother or father – met either socially or at a bereavement support group. Or, you may feel the need for specialized professional help – perhaps no more than a check-up with your doctor for recurrent headaches, perhaps a commitment to some form of therapy for a while.

Choose what you think you need with care and flexibility. Don't hesitate to change if you feel it isn't doing you any good. For example, you don't have to stick with a therapist who makes you feel inadequate in your grief in the hope that it may be doing your soul good. Find people who can give genuine support.

You can also make sure that your other parent knows what help is available – even if he doesn't want to take it up now, there may come a time when, for example, a bereavement support group could help him get back on his feet again. But this is an issue you can't force. When it comes to seeking help, you have to consider your own needs first. In the end, only you can work through your grief, and you are the best person to help yourself.

Being ready for help

This said, the motivation which drives you to ask for help can be complex and delicate. For a while after a death, there may be a strong feeling that others cannot help, even that it is somehow contrary to the nature of your experience to be looking for it. Grief can be so all-embracing that, while you may long to break through it, you may be held back by the fact that you feel so remote from other people, from the happy lack of self-consciousness with which they go about their daily concerns, all unaware of the way your life has been rocked to its depth. You may ask yourself whether it is fair to impose yourself, to ask them to share your shock and devastation.

But, you cannot live for too long with such a strong feeling of being cut off from other people. The fact that it hasn't happened to them can insulate them, as it were, from feeling too much on your behalf – it is always easier to protect yourself from others' sorrow than your own. So, it might be worth taking the plunge if all you want to do is talk.

However, you do need to try and judge what sort of feedback you're going to get. If a friend is absorbed by a new baby, or an aunt is moving house (and, more importantly, if they've never been through grief themselves) they may not be able to give you the in-depth kind of attention you feel you need.

This is when you may need to seek help more actively: and is when readiness comes in. You may need to think about looking for help for some period of time before you can actually bring yourself to act. This is because a move towards help is the beginning of a general move forwards: you may simply have more grieving to do before you can be ready for that.

How can you become ready? There isn't any simple answer. Part of it is allowing yourself sufficient time to grieve; part of it is holding yourself open to the possibility of help as much as possible. Even if you don't want to talk this year, you might be able to do so next year.

Also, your wish for help may come and go. The desire for company on some days may be matched by an equal desire for solitude on others. Your feelings towards others can range from an almost desperate kind of dependence ('I must talk to so-and-so – she's the only one who will understand') to deep anger and indifference. This confusing time is best gone through as lightly as possible, in the sense of not bothering too much about the shifts in your emotions towards others, and what they may think of you. Friends new and old will be there for you when you do become ready for them.

Friends

So, can your existing friends help? Those who still have their parents may not be as supportive as you hope, because they just haven't been through your experience. Hearing about it can be a threat to their own security – it hasn't happened to them yet and naturally they don't want it to. Although they may express some sympathy, it is easy for others to retreat into self-defence, simply to switch off the subject. Besides, it *is* difficult for them to know what to say, or do – although you may always appreciate them making the effort.

> Anita was very touched when an old friend of hers invited her to go on a week's walking tour in the country soon after her mother's death. 'She was the only person who tried to do something solid and practical – she gave up a week of her time. That's the sort of thing you never forget.'

When approaching friends, there is also a danger of draining the same people dry, or of converting them into substitute parents. There may be the temptation to idealize them, or to project on to them fantasies of security which do more properly belong to parents.

> Not wanting to burden her fiancé with her grief too much, Moira got into the habit of calling in on a couple she knew, a few years older than her, who had no children of their own. Even at the time, she realized she was painting a rather rosy picture of them and choosing to ignore their all-too-human characteristics, but she could not help visualizing them as a haven of security, an environment where quarrels rarely took place or were smoothed over with a few wise words! She also realized that her constant visits were beginning to be a strain on two busy people. However, her marriage took place and she moved away before this became too obvious.

The problem here is that just after bereavement is not a very good time for giving in a friendship. With emotional energy absorbed by grief, it is very difficult to take an active, vital part in other inter-changes. You may envy others their 'normality', the fact that they can afford to care about the details of their shopping and their journey to work, when your own normality and balance has been so shattered. In the anguish of grief, the sublime can easily merge into the ridiculous, as Moira recounts.

> I found myself trying to copy the details of their life. I suppose in the hope I could get rid of my uncomfortable feelings and be more like them. I couldn't wait to get married so I'd be happy and settled too. I wanted to buy a house like theirs. I'd even go to Marks & Spencer for food, because they did!

If friends cannot help you evade grief, an existing friend can be a real godsend if he has been through your experience.

> Michael had one good friend of some years' standing, who lost his mother shortly after Michael lost his father. Michael found their talks invaluable in coming to terms with his feelings.

But, just having gone through the same experience isn't always a guarantee of mutual support.

> In theory, Moira and Anita, having met at the hospital where their mothers died, could have made supportive friends for each other. But, if Moira felt envious of her two friends, Anita envied Moira her engagement and the fact that she *was* comparatively settled. Perhaps also they were too similar – both certainly showed a disposition to seek out rather older, mother-type women friends for a while. Besides, neither liked to see each other because of hospital memories this evoked.

Then there are the friends who ignore you, half-consciously, or who put off contacting you from day to day because they don't know what to say. In this case, it may be up to you to get in touch with them. It is hard to have to support uncertain friends with explanations and reassurance, but hopefully you will only need to go through this once. Given that initial frankness from you, they may be emboldened to show much more understanding than you hoped. Friends have their limitations; and they have their own lives to lead. But, try and be open to help if it is offered, and remember that it often comes when you'd expect it least.

Help from a minister

Chapter 7 looked at the way your ideas about the spiritual life and your attitude to the Church might change after a parent's death. Now is a time when you might be tempted to seek support and understanding from one church or another. Yet, many barriers can hold us back from consulting a minister of the Church for guidance during this time: an ingrained opposition to churches; doubt and disbelief; years of neglecting the family religion. The experience of finally plucking up courage to go and discuss your spiritual experience with someone can be disappointing, mundane or even faintly comic.

> Anita, who had been brought up a Catholic but had lapsed in recent years, took to attending a nearby church. Misled by its aura of incense and the regular confessions which took place, she believed it to be Catholic; it wasn't until she found herself face to face with the priest for a heart-to-heart that she realized that it was in fact Anglo-Catholic, very 'high' Church of England. There ensued an embarrassing meeting, during which Anita did her best to extricate herself from the situation without giving offence, and the elderly minister did his best to show how willing he was to help!

Implicit in this story is the demand that the help be of the right sort, and some people are held back from seeking help because, if they were to find it, there would be nothing else to look for. There is perhaps a fear that a reassuring chat with someone seen as possessing superior spiritual nous would be a bit of a let-down; that it would interrupt the spiritual quest which can be part of the painful privilege of grief. Colin was one man who didn't want to be handed answers on a plate.

> I didn't want my grieving tidied up by a man of religion. There were too many loose ends. Besides, it would have deprived me of the chance of going through it alone. More than that, I felt it was something I was meant to go through alone.

However, ministers and priests are just as prey to doubts and fears as lay people, if not more so. They might even argue that a confused struggling with doubt is nearer to spiritual clarity than unquestioning complacence. Certainly, an experienced minister might well be able to point out the ways in which this inner turmoil, this ruthless sorting through of old ideas, can eventually lead to new, stronger ones. There is also the possibility that by sharing your own feelings honestly, you could be helping them to fresh insights on the deepest questions about life and death, which are the bedrock of their existence.

Ministers are there to deal with the questions that may be haunting you: Is there life after death and if so what kind? Are the dead aware of us? Why did your mother or father have to die just then, in that way? What if anything is the value of pain and of unanswered prayers? Even if ministers don't have all the answers, they too may count it as a 'painful privilege' to share your grief for a time.

Using your doctor

As was described in Chapter 4, grief drains your energy and leaves you more liable to illness and hypochondria. Although grief itself is not an illness, it is a very real experience which takes a lot of effort to live through. Bereaved people do become ill more often, especially during the first year. But, the subtle links between mind and body should not mean that you become ashamed of 'imaginary' illnesses; it's more that your resistance to infection is lowered because of the stress of grieving. The links between body and mind are real. Sometimes it is even possible to develop illnesses which mimic that of which the dead parent died – as was mentioned in Chapter 5, Hazel developed stomach and bowel problems, with similar and alarming symptoms to those of her father's disease.

You may well find yourself going to the doctor's more often in the first year or so following your bereavement, for assorted physical ailments and perhaps also for help with your grief-associated emotions. Depending on his personality and experience, your doctor may be able to direct you if, for example, you feel you need counselling. However, bear in mind that you don't have to have a doctor's referral if you prefer to seek out other help yourself.

Another point is that you may want to talk over your parent's illness and death with the doctor, to get straight details which at the time you were too confused to take in properly. Could it have been diagnosed earlier? Was it treated properly? Having such questions answered can not only reassure you and clear your mind; it can also be important in determining your own future health. For example, if your mother died of breast cancer, you might want to pay more particular attention to self-testing and screening; if a father died of heart disease, you could well benefit from checking your own eating and exercise habits.

Trust in your doctor is a major factor in how well you use her during this time – something that may well be more difficult if this was the doctor who was treating your parent. If you don't like your doctor, do weigh up the advantages of her knowing your family history against the possible advantages of a new, more understanding person. But, no matter how sympathetic your doctor may be, don't forget that these days she is pressed for time. So, have a list ready, in case you forget anything, and mention the chief worry which has brought you there – it can be all too easy, when face to face with the presence, to take fright and 'forget' your stupid anxiety that the pain in your chest means incipient heart failure. If you don't come out with it this time, there is the chance that you will have to make several more visits with other symptoms, all masking your chief anxiety. You can be sure that, no matter how silly you may feel talking about your fears, your doctor has heard worse. Besides, giving reassurance is a very valid part of her job; it's not just that she has to do a lot of it, but the simple fact that worry can make you ill. Finally, if you feel you *are* ill, don't assume you are just suffering from grief or that it is 'all in the mind'. If need be, ask for another visit or a second opinion. Make sure you are getting all the medical attention you need.

Looking after yourself

You need to lavish on yourself the same kind of care that you spent (or would have liked to have spent) on your dead parent. This can be hard to do after a death, when it's all too easy to feel that if that's the end that awaits everyone, why bother? Constituted the way we are, however, you will feel better if you do take care of yourself in the here and now. Do this for the sake of others if you can't yet bring yourself to do it for your own sake – for the sake of your other parent, for your friends or for your own family.

Whatever your situation, it is important to be aware of your own value, not to let grief drive you into the ground. The extent to which you care for yourself naturally partly depends on your existing self-esteem, on how good your emotional security has been in the past. For some people it may be more of an effort than for others.

If you have got out of the way of caring for yourself, try and pay yourself little attentions. Treat yourself as you would a special guest. For example, tidiness and cleanliness (or the reverse) are well known for their effects on morale, so it isn't a waste of time to make your surroundings as appealing as possible, even if you live alone. You may well not have the energy for redecorating. But, keeping the house in order, adding some bath essence to your bath, having fresh flowers around can all be little disciplines that help you forwards.

Spending money on yourself can also bring a valuable feeling of release. This doesn't have to be great sums – a new pillow or pair of slippers, a hair-do, some attractive stationery – anything which makes you feel that bit more nurtured. Hoarding money can sometimes be a symptom of hoarding life, of being afraid to move on because your experience of death has cowed you, so do make the effort to splash out sometimes. Also, it can be easy to ignore the broken clock, the worn towels, that you've been living with for months! So, have a look round and see if there are any little ways in which you can minister to yourself or your surroundings.

At some point, when you feel stronger, you may well want to pay the house more fundamental attention. But, don't rush into big, time-consuming projects unless you are very sure that grief is no longer depleting so much of your energy.

The importance of eating and resting properly should be stressed again here. Try not to indulge in too many comfort habits, such as eating chocolate – easy to slip into at such a time. Or if you do, at least make sure you have eaten a well-balanced meal first. Do bother to cook for yourself, even though a dislike of food can be a part of grief.

Hazel, for example, felt as if everything she ate were cotton wool, and lost a stone in the months after her father's death. She was helped by a friend who suggested she eat small but healthy meals – nothing but fresh fruit and vegetables; pure, unfatty protein such as chicken or fish; brown rice, and wholemeal bread.

More addictive habits could also be mentioned here, such as alcohol, with grief paving the way to dependence, especially if there was a dependent relationship with the dead parent, and/or a well-established drinking habit before (see Nicholas's story in Chapter 6). What could be emphasized here, however, is the danger to health this poses: the fact that both heavy drinking and smoking stand in the way of good eating habits and more than pave the way to further disease. Recognizing this is one thing, however; battling against a well-established habit or an addiction quite another. Recognizing when you need help here can be vital, so if you feel you can't do it alone, don't be ashamed to ask (see below and Useful addresses).

Bereavement and other support groups

There are a number of bereavement organizations and support groups. You may need to look at more than one organization before finding one that suits you; don't give up if you try one, find it unsympathetic and decide it isn't for you. There may be another not far away where the format is slightly different or where you feel more at ease with the people. While bereavement *is* a great leveller, it is only sensible to look round for a group you feel at home with if you can. Some people also find that they only need one or two visits – just to know they are not unique, that their rocketing emotions are normal, can be reassurance enough.

The Useful addresses section of this book gives the headquarters of national support organizations. You may also be able to find local bereavement groups; ask at your doctor's surgery, the library, or your local Citizens Advice Bureau. The bereavement service will be able to put you in touch either with other people who've had your experience or with a counsellor, specifically trained to deal with the 'complications' of mourning.

Sometimes, it can be difficult to disentangle grief from a whole host of other emotions or life-problems. In this case you may also want to go to a group which deals specifically with your problem. If one doesn't exist why not start one yourself? This doesn't mean such a group has to be attended for the rest of your life – use it at your discretion, and don't hesitate to move on when you feel ready. The ultimate aim of going to any group is to discover the sources of inner strength that enable you to move towards true adult independence. Some people also find satisfaction in eventually contributing to such groups as a leader or organizer of some kind, or as a lay or trained counsellor.

Stocktaking

Some people feel the urge to write down what has happened to them, especially if it has been a harrowing or violent death. This can indeed be a way of making sense of the event, of finding order in what might otherwise appear to be random suffering.

> Clare, in her early 20s, nursed both her parents through cancer and saw them die within weeks of each other. About 18 months after their deaths, she began to write a novel about her harrowing experience. It came out with no holds barred and, while she eventually realized she couldn't publish it, she never doubted the value of having written such a painful testimony.

While this kind of stocktaking can be helpful in attempting to put the death in its place in your life, there's no doubt that it does demand stamina. However, it is also the kind of project which seems more daunting beforehand than afterwards; though it may cost you some pain, the end result can be the new strength which comes from having purged your memory. Another bonus is increased self-knowledge.

> While writing, Clare found that along with her altruistic act in nursing her parents, she experienced many bitter feelings. 'It wasn't all a warm glow of satisfaction that I was doing the right thing.' She had to come to terms with many unsatisfactory elements in her relationship with both parents – in other words, she wasn't just writing the history of the illness, but the history of all their lives.

It may not be possible to look at your parent's illness and death in isolation – you may have to look at the way family relationships have contributed to the way you are, and aspects of your life and character you feel guilty or unhappy about. Getting these down in black-and-white can really help clear the ground for new growth. But, it's important to know your own strength before you embark on this – not too soon after the death, when you may still be too raw to handle such material. The aim of such a project is not to be hard on yourself. Don't worry about it being a work of art – one idea is to do it in note form, on small index cards, bit by bit as you feel like it. It's also a good idea to have a physical project on at the same time, such as re-digging the garden – not only do you need this to counteract your mental work, memories do come to you while you're absorbed in manual work. We tend to block out unpleasant details, even if we believe we'll never forget at the time. You may need to take weeks over your stocktaking for all the memories to drift back.

In memoriam

One of the strongest needs felt after death is to keep in touch somehow with the person who has died, and this can actually be very helpful in determining the course of your grief. For example, some people feel that care of the grave is a chance to do a last service for their dead parent: to smooth over any last little misunderstandings; to make good any past little defects in attention or to act simply out of respect for their memory, as a reassurance that someone once so important will not be forgotten if they can help it. Go to any cemetery at the weekend and you can see people carrying watering cans, trowels and new plants to the grave of their loved one.

This can be a time when you begin to understand the value of traditional ways of paying respect to the dead, from looking after the grave to lighting candles or arranging for requiem masses to be said. However, these channels may not seem right for you. You may want to do more: to make your own personal contribution to your parent's memory; or to do so with another family member.

Michael planted a tree at Tom's graveside and visited regularly to take care of it, sometimes on his own and sometimes with a brother. Hazel, whose father died of cancer, made an annual contribution to a cancer research charity in his memory; she also met her mother at the grave once a month, to tend it, or just to stand there for a few minutes.

Other family

Some people have found other family a great source of help when it comes to the long-term appraisal of grief and the relationship with dead parents.

Moira and her grandmother had always been close as she had helped bring her up when Moira's mother had gone back to work. She was able to share all the knowledge of Moira's mother, and of Moira's early years, and so was a great source of consolation. Two of Guy's father's cousins visited from Australia. Guy felt it was satisfying to see their family resemblance to Edward and to feel that they'd come partly to pay tribute to his memory.

Some way into grief, you may long for people to talk about your dead father or mother with – people who knew them well. Family are often the nearest source of information, even if you sometimes have to distinguish between reality and family myth.

What doesn't help

In the tenderness of early bereavement, you are more vulnerable to stray comments from other people, be they negative or positive. While it helps to be aware of this increased sensitivity, you should also be able to trust your instincts in sorting out the sheep from the goats – in deciding for yourself what is not helpful and in protecting yourself from it as much as possible.

Perhaps the most demoralizing attitude is that which preaches the 'stiff upper lip', which seems to accuse the grieving person of self-pity and moral 'flabbiness'. It's an attitude which advises you to pull yourself together and get on with it, that there are plenty of other people in the world who are worse off than you – a view which ignores the quality of your grief in order to focus on false estimates of quantity. Just as bad, if more cloying, is the view that everything happens for the best and that God has a plan for your life which you will be able to appreciate only later. This is a kind of sentimentalizing of the much tougher fact that a parent's death does pull you forward willy-nilly into new growth.

A word of warning: be very cautious about seeking consolation in two potentially harmful areas. One is via spiritualism (seances or other means) which promises to get in touch with the dead. Apart from anything else, this can be psychologically negative, turning the clock backwards in the grieving process. Whether you can see it or not, time moves slowly forwards to the point where you can begin life anew. The second area is that of new, alternative religions or cults: beware of those which offer instant answers or those which demand that you give money or leave home to move in with other members. As always, it is up to you to decide on the type and quality of help which appears to be on offer.

10

Getting on with your life

Grief must not become a refuge from life. Impossible though it may seem in the shocked beginning, people can sometimes slip into the way of holding on to grief. Apart from anything else, there is perhaps an unspoken fear of 'getting on with living' because it brings us nearer to the point at which our own parent died. Fear of death leads to fear of life.

But, at some point, you do have to start living again. Maybe there is a marriage waiting, perhaps study plans were postponed for a time in order to be with the bereaved parent, or a house move. Whatever it is, it will need to be tackled, especially if grief is becoming an excuse for not getting on with life.

Sometimes it isn't that easy. You know the next step, you want to take it, but you linger where you are, postponing that inevitable next move until driven to it by the discomfort of your present position. We can easily acquire habits in grief, just as in other life situations – habits of staying in and not socializing, habits of rushing round to be with our other parent, or of talking only to the same few people. After a while, there can be safety in unhappiness. It can be painful to leave the familiar behind – even familiar pain.

Generally, you know for yourself when an old mode of living begins to go stale. You feel bored and restless, and your mind starts making plans almost independently. Sometimes the date for moving on is set for you: a new job to go to, for example, or the birth of a baby. It is more difficult when you don't feel that inner urge to move on; when motivation is lacking or you can't seem to fix your goals. There is also your other parent to be considered as you make plans for the future. How closely should your lives be interlinked? How far should you assume responsibility for her well-being? When do you need to be selfish? How can you find a compromise between family and your own personal needs?

Sometimes it is only after a parent's death that we begin to think for ourselves. Perhaps for the first time we have to define an identity independently of family. If this process is long or convoluted, the result can be an increased, enduring inner strength.

When to start again?

It can take years to work through a parent's death; years before you may feel your life is back on course. Hopefully you will avoid denigrating this time as meaningless or a waste, however troubled and bleak it may be at times. The rate at which you are able to take more interest in your future partly depends on which stage of your life your parent died. If it was at an early or difficult stage, when your plans or identity may have been more tenuous, it is all going to take longer.

> Guy was a case in point; his father died when Guy was 21, at a time of transition in his life. He was finishing his studies without definite plans for the future. This lack of clarification was amplified by Guy's own rather diffident character and the extent to which he had been subconsciously relying on Edward to point him in the right direction after university. Guy felt it actually wasn't until he reached his early 30s that he really felt settled in life.

This can happen to anyone; the '20s' are traditionally a time of experiment and of identity-seeking. Guy's story also shows that your own character and outlook play a part in how long you take to find your way after a parent's death. For example, someone who had strong ideas about a career-path might have had more of an anchor in life.

You also need to differentiate between fully working through the implications of a parent's death (something which sometimes is never finished) and coming through the worst of grief. Although this may take place over a two-year period, grief may also lighten after six months or a year. Even if you still have a major amount of grieving to do, the first impact of sorrow may melt away enough for you to feel you can be getting on with life.

Getting 'stuck' in grief

What if you feel you can't move on? If you've been at a certain stage in grief for some time you may not see when it's going to end. It is possible to become 'stuck' in grief – to go through life in a kind of 'settled depression'; to have been so cowed by the death that you no longer have the confidence or will to make plans or achieve enjoyment.

You need to be gentle on yourself and lower your self-expectations. Don't feel, for example, that you should put the event behind you or that you should have recovered by now. It may simply be a case of grief taking up more of your time than you could have anticipated. Generally, though, if after two years you feel that your grief has not lightened significantly, it would be wise to seek external help if you have not already done so (see Chapter 9).

Prolonged grief can be part of other personality or life difficulties. Sometimes it can be hard to disentangle grief from these. Alternatively, the consequences of your parent's death may have unleashed life-situations which entail a whole host of other emotions – maybe your life has been slowed down or your plans changed by your parent's death. For example, it can be difficult to disentangle sorrow at your loss from other sources of misery, such as loneliness and the longing for a partner, or deep dissatisfaction with your job. This is where help comes in: outside stimulus and feedback can help you identify more accurately all the aspects of your life about which you don't feel happy. Hopefully, this can spur you into taking steps to amend these feelings.

Another source of pain can be when your parent does not progress in grief, or when your sorrow does not keep pace with his. You may need to distinguish between the grief of others and of yourself, if the time comes when you feel that it's healthier for you to move on. However, here you need to distinguish between your opinion of your parent's grief and its real nature. Guilt at wanting to move on could be leading you to exaggerate it.

Letting your other parent go

Naturally, your surviving parent is going to be a prime consideration when you think about getting on with your life. But, does he or she really depend on you as much as you might think? Or is it your own sense of responsibility and perhaps guilt which partly makes you reluctant to move on? This can be particularly strong if you're single and not yet committed to buying your own home.

> Guy, who had been about to move into a shared flat when his father died, stayed at home with his mother and more or less postponed his life for two years. He felt it would be awkward if he got a girlfriend and tended to hurry home immediately after work, rarely going out for a drink with his colleagues. He also felt it would be hard on his mother if he changed jobs, as he wanted to, and perhaps had to move. In the end, a new job and a girl appeared on the scene at around the same time, just as Guy was getting thoroughly depressed with his supportive role. He moved in with his girlfriend in another town and, rather to his surprise, his mother coped very well.

Letting your life revolve around your parent, perhaps even being a substitute partner, isn't much fun for you, even though you have the satisfaction of knowing you've done your duty. If allowed to continue for too long, it can become a means of hiding from life. Sometimes it may not be much fun for your parent, either – the last thing your parent may want is a sympathetic adult child hanging around if, for example, he or she is trying to forge a new relationship!

> Guy's mother was really quite relieved when he left as she now felt free to get on with her life. She knew she'd been holding Guy back and that this was against the natural flow of life. She was also beginning to feel a need for more privacy and freedom. She was able to build quite a good social life after he left and eventually decided to re-marry.

If one parent dies relatively young, as Guy's father did (at 47), re-marriage is more of a possibility. But even if this isn't likely or never happens, your parent needs to be free to rearrange his own life – that rebuilding of a daily routine. In many ways, grief is a re-learning process; your other parent has to acquire so many new habits if he is living alone – from making tea and shopping, to planning holidays and making new friends.

If you already have a partner or family of your own, the situation is different, but you also have to consider how far your other parent should be involved in your future plans. Would it be healthier to have more of a break, or could you accommodate closer contact? For example, after some time has gone by, you may want to re-examine the old question of your all living together, or of creating a 'granny flat' if circumstances permit.

> Moira and her husband John got into the habit of having her father round for lunch every Sunday. Moira would also pop in once or twice a week to take him food and do a bit of ironing or cleaning. This was fine for about 18 months, but then Moira and John decided they wanted to start a family. This meant moving to a larger house in a more rural area. However, they did have qualms about how Moira's father would manage. They felt he had become dependent on them and that it had perhaps been a mistake to do so much for him. Moira left it until she became pregnant and then explained the situation to him. She and John had decided that they could manage if her father chose to live with them. In the event he refused, saying they needed to live their own lives, and that it was time he made more of an effort for himself.

This decision was probably a bit of a relief all round, though tinged with sadness. Moira's father, however, having had more experience of new babies than Moira, was being realistic – something Moira came to appreciate when in due course she did have a child of her own! It really is a question of finding a balance between your own needs, and those of your other parent – this balance won't ever be quite perfect. If you do decide to move, as Moira did, there may be residues of guilt and feelings that you've abandoned your other parent. However, as Moira's father seemed to feel instinctively, such a move can be healthy in terms of forcing the parent who's left to face life more actively.

Alternatively, it may seem natural to arrange for your parent to live with you, although probably more so if you have a large amount of space.

> Sara made a different decision with her mother when her father died – she invited her to move in. But, circumstances were different – Sara owned a large house in the country with adjacent stables. Her mother occupied her own flat within the house but had what amounted to a job – helping Sara with her three children, shopping, and coping with the girls who came for riding holidays. This arrangement pleased all parties.

Your older parent

This is the question which looms ever bigger the longer you progress through life – what is the best way of ensuring care for an older parent who may no longer be able to care for himself? The full implications of this question go well beyond the scope of this book (see Further reading). As a starting point, you'll need to consider how close the fit can be between your parent's personality and his lifestyle – and how much help you are willing and able to give towards that lifestyle.

For example, if your father is an independent man who would loathe 'a home' or sheltered accommodation, are you willing to pop in when needed or would it be more appropriate to delegate some of it? How much help are your local social services willing or able to give? Is your ageing parent likely to need nursing? Can you deal with the forgetfulness and hostility associated with some conditions such as dementia and senility? Last but by no means least is your parent's own attitude. As with a dying parent, the care you offer has to be conditioned by how much he or she is willing to accept. However, it is possible to reach acceptable compromises.

> Philip, 79, had always relished standing on his own two feet, but age had greatly slowed him down. While he was not a danger to himself, he could only move about slowly and really needed a wheelchair to reach the local shops. He moved to a complex of one-bedroom bungalows which had been discretely fitted out for older people, with alarm cords in case of trouble. This was just a few miles away from his daughter,

Rebecca, who was able to visit three times a week, a home-help calling on the other days.

In this case, both parties felt they needed to keep their distance a little in order to maintain some privacy and independence. But what about those who find the call to duty is that much more compelling, who feel that only living with a parent will do? This situation, which has its dangers, is considered next.

Disguised dependency

The old maid who stays at home to look after her ageing parents isn't just a cliché of recent British history. Though less common, it does still happen, and there is a special kind of reaction to the loss of parents you've spent years looking after.

> Jean never left home. She stayed to care for her father during his last illness, and after that to look after her mother when her father died. Jean was eventually left a very angry middle-aged spinster when her mother's turn came to die. Jean felt that not only was there now no one to do the same for her, but also, in spite of their apparent dependence, her parents had always run her life and were continuing to do so, even though dead.

The days are gone when it was taken for granted that women gave up marriage and a career for ageing parents. With these changed expectations, the legacy that's left behind after the death of parents you've spent years looking after can be bitter. You may feel frustration, loneliness, and the feeling of having wasted life in useless sacrifice. It is all the harder to strike out anew if the habit of many years of care is behind you. Extra help may be needed to come to terms with the many negative feelings that such a situation can produce. Jean, for example, started going to a bereavement support group. She also went for counselling for an intensive two-year period in which she was able to rebuild her sense of her own value.

Jean's story illustrates why it is so important to move on – not to become stuck in a situation which can take years of your life and which later you can but regret. However, there is no need for attitudes to your parents to be totally polarized, as Jean herself points out.

> I was too black-and-white, too either–or. I thought, *either* I'm heartless, if I leave them and go off and live my own life – *or* I'm selfless, loving and doing the Christian thing if I stay at home. There were just those two alternatives and nothing else, for years. It never occurred to me,

say, to get myself a little studio flat down the road, so I'd have my own space but still be able to pop in and see them every day. Or even just to go out twice a week – I could have met someone that way, married, and still looked after them. I didn't think of it. It just seemed like they needed me and that was that. Going to a group and talking to people has expanded my ideas – after the event, unfortunately.

In other words, compromise may involve some pain on one side or another, but this can be secondary to the deeper needs which are urging a person on into life.

This isn't to condemn all living-together arrangements out of hand. But there is a vast difference between a carefully considered invitation to a parent to move in with you, and Jean's case, where she simply never left the nest.

If you do want an older parent to live with you, practical and emotional questions need to be considered very much side-by-side. Will your parent need a downstairs room to avoid stairs? Are there children around whose needs might clash with his? Is your parent going to contribute rent or will you be budgeting for extra food, heating and washing facilities? It is as well to get all such points clear beforehand, to make sure you understand the full extent to which you're committing yourself.

Leaving the nest again: goals

The releasing of emotional energy which comes from moving on is not something you should deny yourself. You even need to leave living parents behind to some extent in order to mature. However, bereavement is a great shaker of confidence, so you may have to make efforts to regain any that you have lost. Setting goals can help give valuable restructuring to a life devastated by grief, so long as you feel ready to move on. It's an important process because it involves a change in thinking patterns which is as profound as the change called for previously in grief. From considering endings, you now have to consider beginnings again. The structure in which happy planning was possible has been destroyed – you need to build a new structure before you can plan again. However, the setting of goals in itself can help you to become ready, and achieving a certain number of smaller goals can help you towards bigger decisions.

Hazel started her hunt for a new job by having her hair done. Michael was disciplined about taking it bit by bit when it came to moving house, a project which seemed overwhelming before it was begun.

Whether you call this the 'slice of salami' technique (after modern time-management programmes) or 'one day at a time' (as in some self-help groups) the principle is the same: don't agitate yourself by thinking about all the future possibilities. Don't try to visualize the end result, but to do what you can, right here and now, to bring you one small step nearer to your goal. Don't forget that that goal can simply be peaceful living on a daily basis – it doesn't have to be anything spectacular.

Nonetheless, what about those important long-term goals? Because the fact of death may have reversed plans for living, it can be difficult to get in touch with your real aims in life again. You may feel you can't think of anything you'd really like to achieve. It could simply be that you've 'forgotten' – sorrow has driven it from your mind. One method of getting back in touch with your inner goals is meditating or day-dreaming – allowing your mind to wander through all the possibilities. Give yourself permission to consider the wild, the fantastic and the impossible – you never know, it might just become fact if you choose to direct your energies in that direction! Sometimes circumstances shift very quickly, leaving you to face the real possibility of realizing what has for years been a vague dream. The circumstances can be material, but needn't be.

> Michael had always wanted to start his own business but felt tied to his job. This goal seemed even more remote after Tom's death, when he felt he barely had the motivation to crawl through his present job. A year or so after Tom's death, however, a redundancy payment gave him just enough capital to realize his ambition.

> Guy desperately wanted to buy his own flat – a simple enough aim, but one which seemed fraught with complications; partly because he felt his mother still needed him, partly because of the stasis of grief. In his case, moving towards his goal was a simple matter of realizing one day that there was nothing to stop him.

The problem isn't really one of possibility or impossibility – it's to do with the dynamics of seeing 'dream becoming reality' and of facing up to the inescapable disappointments entailed: the banality of losing something to wish for. Having your dream become fact in itself entails loss.

However gradually or quickly you choose to move, the depth of thinking remains the same – a profound decision has been made to change, to move on. In many ways this is a decision which makes itself over a period of time although you can help it along, mainly by looking after yourself and by seeking, and using, what support is available.

Although this decision may grow slowly, beneath the surface with many months of inner preparation, it can sometimes manifest itself suddenly. Some people seem to operate better by taking a flying leap into the future, even though this may not cut all your difficulties away completely.

> Anita, who spent several months at home, felt at first that her presence did have some value for her father, but soon felt she was just hanging around. She wanted to go back to India, where she had travelled extensively a few years back, but simply couldn't break the pattern of work and home. 'More than that, I couldn't seem to remember or imagine any other life – it was as if all the colour had faded from my memories, if you like. I suppose it was a kind of depression.' However, when she realized how pervading was the sense of greyness in her life, she decided she had nothing to lose, and left. Once away, her only regret was that she hadn't done it before, saving herself months of bleak indecision.

Of course, one does have to distinguish here between the genuine need to move on and the temptation to escape. Such a move need not be a running away from necessary pain.

> Anita found that there were still painful days, when she could spend hours crying. However, the release and stimulus of going away actually seemed to help her get in touch better with her grief. 'I liked being alone in a foreign country, I did feel more free from restraint – whether that was good or bad, I don't know. I felt more alive – that I could accommodate grief better. Before, the dullness of the life I'd been leading had stopped me feeling anything at all.'

This is also an example of the way people sometimes need to create their own circumstances in which to come to terms with grief. As said before, it may not solve everything – residual problems may still need to be faced on coming home – but this 'weaving of protection' can be valuable in giving strength until the reality of a situation can be faced on home ground once more.

The lifting of grief

It could be that Anita, who departed some two years after her mother's death, was experiencing a lifting of grief – in which the main body of sorrow isn't as dark and overwhelming, but in which pain can and does return at intervals. Other life events can, in retrospect, be seen to trigger this lifting of grief, too.

Michael and his wife had a third child almost two years after Tom's death. This was a more than ordinarily emotive event for Michael, but he found that his regret at Tom's not being there to see his new grandchild was softened by a new acceptance of what had happened.

Incidentally, a death is said to be one of the most common reasons there is for a pregnancy – an urge as it were to defeat death by bringing a new life into the world.

Grief can depart more unobtrusively. Moira, for example, found that it went little by little, under the pressure of everyday business – shopping, cooking and preparing for a baby. One morning she woke up and realized she just hadn't thought about her mother for a couple of weeks.

Some people are worried that this constitutes a kind of disloyalty to their mother or father; Michael was especially concerned at how impossible it was to hang on to the purity of any emotion and at how soon it was trampled underfoot by ordinary life. He realized, however, that to try and hang on to grief would have been less natural than this forgetting and that it was possible to honour his father's memory without the anguish of grief.

> In the beginning, I'd break down and cry; my mother would say, 'Time, give it time,' and I'd say, 'No, no, you don't understand . . .' Now, three years later, I can drive past my father's old house without really noticing it. And I feel rather sorry in a way – losing that grief.

However, this brings us to the final point to be considered when it comes to re-starting your life: the old adage that time heals, however unbelievable this seems in the beginning. The force of life does carry you on, like it or not; second-by-second new thoughts, new impressions come, causing you to drift ever further away from your original overwhelming grief. Part of the value of grieving fully is how much more bearable, even comfortable, your feelings become once you've lived through your sorrow.

As Michael pointed out, the lifting of grief is yet another kind of loss. You lose touch with the emotions that were such a powerful link with your dead mother or father. It can be at this point that you begin to realize the value of your experience in grief as the painful tribute paid to love.

Useful addresses

Age UK
207–221 Pentonville Road
London N1 9UZ
Advice line: 0800 169 6565
Website: www.ageuk.org.uk

Aims to improve later life for everyone through information and support.

The British Association for Counselling and Psychotherapy
BACP House
15 St John's Business Park
Lutterworth LE17 4HB
Tel.: 01455 883300
Fax: 01455 550243
Website: www.bacp.co.uk

Carers UK
20 Great Dover Street
London SE1 4LX
Tel.: 020 7378 4999
Advice line: 0808 808 7777 (10 a.m. to 12 noon and 2 to 4 p.m.,
Wednesday and Thursday)
Fax: 020 7378 9781
Website: www.carersuk.org

Crossroads Caring for Carers (Northern Ireland)
7 Regent Street
Newtownards
County Down BT23 4AB
Northern Ireland
Tel.: 028 9181 4455
Website: www.crossroadscare.co.uk

Crossroads Caring Scotland
24 George Square
Glasgow G2 1EG
Tel.: 0141 226 3793
Website: www.crossroads-scotland.co.uk

Cruse Bereavement Care
PO Box 800
Richmond
Surrey TW9 1RG
Tel.: 020 8939 9530
Daytime helpline: 0844 477 9400
Young person's helpline: 0808 808 1677 (9.30 a.m. to 5 p.m., Monday to Friday)
Website: www.crusebereavementcare.org.uk

Help the Hospices
Hospice House
34–44 Britannia Street
London WC1X 9JG
Tel.: 020 7520 8200
Fax: 020 7278 1021
Website: www.helpthehospices.org.uk

Irish Hospice Foundation
Morrison Chambers (4th floor)
32 Nassau Street
Dublin 2
Republic of Ireland
Tel.: (01) 6793188
Fax: (01) 6730040
Website: www.hospice-foundation.ie

St Christopher's Hospice
51–59 Lawrie Park Road
Sydenham
London SE26 6DZ
Tel.: 020 8768 4500
Fax: 020 8659 8680
Website: www.stchristophers.org.uk

Other organizations

Admiral Nursing DIRECT: tel.: 0800 888 6678 (helpline staffed by Admiral Nurses trained in dementia care; 11 a.m. to 8.45 p.m., Tuesday and Thursday; 10 a.m. to 1 p.m., Saturday); website: https://www. dementiauk.org/get-support/admiral-nursing/

Alzheimer's Research Trust: tel.: 0300 111 5555; website: www. alzheimers-research.org.uk

Alzheimer's Society: National Dementia Helpline: 0300 222 1122 (8.30 a.m. to 6.30 p.m., Monday to Friday); website: www.alzheimers.org.uk

Care Choices: tel.: 01223 207770; website: www.carechoices.co.uk; for information about available care options

Care Quality Commission: tel.: 03000 616161 (8.30 a.m. to 5.30 p.m., Monday to Friday); website: www.cqc.org.uk; offers advice on choosing social care

Citizens Advice: helpline: 03444 111 444; website: www.citizensadvice. org.uk

Dementia UK: tel.: 0800 888 6678; website: www.dementiauk.org; dedicated to improving the quality of life for people with dementia

Disabled Living Foundation: tel.: 020 7289 6111 (9 a.m. to 5 p.m., Monday to Friday); helpline: 0300 999 0004 (10 a.m. to 4 p.m., Monday to Friday); website: www.dlf.org.uk; offers advice on equipment to help those with special needs

Macmillan Cancer Support: tel.: 0808 808 0000 (8 a.m. to 8 p.m. daily); website: www.macmillan.org.uk

Motor Neurone Disease (MND) Association: tel.: 01604 250505; MND Connect Helpline: 0808 802 6262 (advice, practical and emotional support and directing to other services and agencies); website: www. mndassociation.org

Natural Death Centre: helpline: 01962 712690; website: www.naturaldeath. org.uk; provides information on Advance Directives or Living Wills

Office of the Public Guardian: tel.: 0300 456 0300; website: https://www. gov.uk/government/organisations/office-of-the-public-guardian; offers information about Powers of Attorney and the Court of Protection

Relatives' and Residents' Association: helpline: 020 7359 8136 (9.30 a.m. to 1 p.m., Monday to Friday); website: www.relres.org; provides support with and information about going into residential care

Samaritans: helpline: 116 123; website: www.samaritans.org

Turn2us: website: https://www.turn2us.org.uk/get-support/Turn2us-Funds/Turn2us-Elizabeth-Finn-Fund; formerly known as Elizabeth Finn Care, Turn2us provides grants for families in need

WPF Therapy: tel.: 020 7378 2000; website: www.wpf.org.uk

Further reading

Ainsworth-Smith, Ian and Speck, Peter. *Letting Go – Caring for the Dying and Bereaved*. SPCK, London, 1982.

Alexander, Helen (ed.). *Living with Dying*. Broadcasting Support Services, London, 1990.

Beauvoir, Simone de. *A Very Easy Death*. Penguin, Harmondsworth, 1969.

Cohen, David. *Aftershock: The Psychological and Political Consequences of Disaster*. Paladin Grafton Books, London, 1991.

Doyle, Derek. *A Dying Relative*. Macdonald, Edinburgh, 1983.

Duda, Deborah. *Coming Home: A Guide to Dying at Home with Dignity*. Aurora Press, New York, 1987.

Eisenhauer, Jane (ed.). *Traveller's Tales: Poetry from Hospice*. Marshal Pickering, London, 1989.

Hinton, John. *Dying*. Penguin, Harmondsworth, 1967 and 1972.

Hollins, Sheila and Sireling, Lester. *When Mum Died and When Dad Died*. St George's Hospital Medical School, London (in association with Silent Books, Cambridge, for adults with learning difficulties or children), 1989.

Kübler-Ross, Elisabeth. *On Death and Dying*. Tavistock Publications, London, 1970.

Lake, Tony. *Living with Grief*. Sheldon Press, London, 1984.

Lewis, C. S. *A Grief Observed*. Faber & Faber, London, 1961 and 1985.

Muir, J. A. and McKenzie, Heather. *Caring For Older People*. Penguin, Harmondsworth, 1986.

Murray Parkes, Colin. *Bereavement. Studies of Grief in Adult Life*. Penguin, Harmondsworth, 1972 and 1983.

Owens, Dr R. G. and Naylor, F. G. P. *Living While Dying*. Thorsons, Wellingborough, 1989.

Pulling, Jenny. *The Caring Trap*. Fontana, London, 1987.

Richardson, Jean. *A Death in the Family*. Lion, Oxford, 1979 and 1982.

Stedeford, Averil. *Facing Death*. Heinemann, London, 1984.

Wallbank, Susan. *Bereavement in Young Adults*. CRUSE Publications, London, 1991.

Wells, Rosemary. *Helping Children Cope with Grief*. Sheldon Press, London, 2007.

Whitaker, A. (ed.). *All in the End is Harvest – An Anthology for Those who Grieve*. Darton, Longman & Todd in association with CRUSE, London, 1984.

Winn, D. *The Hospice Way*. Optima, London, 1987.

Worden, J. William. *Grief Counselling and Grief Therapy*. Tavistock Publications, London, 1983.

Index